IBSS 1991

Banking Operations in a Changing Environment: The Profitable Use of Resources

The Chartered
Institute
of Bankers

10 Lombard Street, London EC3V 9AS

i

First published in 1991

BANKERS BOOKS LIMITED
c/o The Chartered Institute of Bankers
10 Lombard Street
London EC3V 9AS

CIB Publications are published by The Chartered Institute of Bankers, a non-profit making registered educational charity, and are distributed exclusively by Bankers Books Limited which is a wholly-owned subsidiary of The Chartered Institute of Bankers.

British Library Cataloguing in Publication Data
A catalogue record for this book is available from the British Library

ISBN 0 85297 304 7

Typeset in Plantin 10/12pt by Proset Photocomp Ltd, Canterbury
Text printed on 100gsm white cartridge, cover on 250gsm art
Printed by KPC Group, Ashford

Contents

Director's Foreword

From time to time in the last 12 months, I have wondered whether we had chosen the right theme — banking is now such a fast-moving business — but two recent observations convinced me that we had.

First, a comment by one of the speakers: "very often, the people who prevent banks from losing money do not receive as much reward as those who make it — though the former can contribute just as much to the viability of a bank over the long run"; and then by the Institute's own Librarian: "the marketing manuals have lost their glamour — everyone wants books on risk now". In using the word "operations" in the title, I had partly in mind this less glamorous side of the business, and the use of BankExec, as a result of one more successful bit of Anglo-US co-operation, will emphasize a lot of important messages.

Of course, all our authors have truly global responsibilities, and their opinions are sought by a much wider audience than the 250 or so bankers from 60 countries who took part in the 44th IBSS in Cambridge in 1991. That is why this book is being published, and I should like to thank everyone for their efforts in getting it out in such good time.

Eric Glover
Director, 44th IBSS
Secretary-General, The Chartered Institute of Bankers

v

Banking in a Changing World Economy

The Rt Hon
Robin Leigh-Pemberton, FCIB
*Governor of the Bank
of England*

1

The Rt Hon Robin Leigh-Pemberton, FCIB

Born in 1927 and educated at Eton College, Robin Leigh-Pemberton read classics at Trinity College, Oxford after military service with the Grenadier Guards. He was called to the Bar in 1954 and practised law until 1960.

He joined the board of National Westminster Bank in 1972, becoming deputy chairman in 1974, and chairman in 1977, a position he held until he was appointed Governor of the Bank of England for a five-year term from 1 July 1983. He has subsequently been reappointed for a further five years.

Mr. Leigh-Pemberton has been a member of the National Economic Development Council since 1982. He was Pro-Chancellor of the University of Kent from 1977-83, when an Honorary Doctorate of Civil Law was conferred on him.

After serving as Vice Lord Lieutenant of Kent for 10 years, he succeeded Lord Astor as Lord Lieutenant of Kent in 1982. He was appointed to the Privy Council in 1987.

Contents

Introduction

Among the developed countries some, like the UK, have recently been in recession and others are growing more slowly than in recent years. Whether this amounts to a world recession is a matter of semantics, and may, fortunately, not be something which needs to be resolved, since it does appear that the worst may soon be over. Even so, projected growth among industrial countries of, say, 1% this year would, after the brisk performance of the middle and late 1980s, be a salutary reminder that the economic cycle has not entirely been vanquished, while regrettably the gulf between the developed and the developing countries remains as wide as ever.

Bearing in mind that the overall theme set for this year's School is *Banking Operations in a Changing Environment — The Profitable Use of Resources*, the first part of this paper addresses a number of recent developments of potential significance for the world economy, before going on to say something about the economic outlook itself. The second part of the paper discusses some of the challenges which face banks in the present financial and economic environment.

1. Developments in the World Economy

Demise of the Command Economy

The first economic development considered here is the widespread, dramatic and historic collapse of the "command" economies of the previously so-called Eastern Bloc, and the associated moves towards more democratic government and market-oriented economic policies in those countries.

The challenges facing them are enormous. Adjustment is bound to be painful, as is already evident. But the prospective eventual rewards should provide the incentive to persevere. The benefits which structural reform and a stabilising macro-economic policy environment can bring, have been seen recently in countries such as Chile and Mexico; and, although the transition from decades under a communist system may present problems of a considerably greater magnitude and complexity than those experienced recently in Latin America, there should be no doubts about the great economic potential which the reforms, if properly managed, should eventually unleash.

The burden of adjustment will of course fall on the eastern countries themselves. Transition to a market-based economy necessarily involves sharp changes in relative prices and considerable upheaval at the work-place, with inevitably higher unemployment, at least over the short term. The prospective need for resources is such that the countries must at least sustain — and preferably improve — the rate of savings domestically, as well as providing a hospitable environment for foreign investors in political, legal and fiscal terms. (This, of course, applies to developing countries more generally.)

But the West can help. Although there is not much existing economic interdependence between East and West — in terms of trade flows for instance — the policies of the West will probably have an important bearing on developments in the East. Most of all, the attainment of steady, non-inflationary growth in the West will provide the environment most conducive to the development of economic links with the East and expansion in Eastern Europe itself. Liberal trade regimes giving proper market access for eastern products will be essential too.

Businesses in the UK and other developed countries — including banks — should be alert to the opportunities which may exist or develop, and which certainly will arise if reform proves successful. This is not to suggest that businesses and banks should make major commitments immediately; but it would be foolish for anyone to close their mind to business links with the eastern part of Europe.

Of most immediate relevance, however, is the paramount need for structural reform; in particular, the need to establish a legal framework of adequate contract and property laws, a proper accounting system, and a banking system that can be effective in channelling resources from savers to worthwhile projects. These developments must be paralleled by the development of a price mechanism that responds to shifts in the pattern of supply and demand and a framework of macro-economic stability. Without progress on all these fronts, money from the West would be of little use. But, so far as technical assistance is concerned, both the private sectors and the governments of the West can make a vital contribution right now.

GEMU

The collapse of communism has touched the West — and particularly the European Community — most directly through the economic and monetary unification of Germany. Against a background of impending crisis and mass migration from the former GDR to the FRG, this was

6

implemented with astonishing rapidity. The immediate costs have been high, as is witnessed by severe unemployment in the former GDR and the mounting cost to the Federal budget. There are therefore inevitably those who argue that the situation should have been addressed differently. But there were really bound to be high adjustment costs in transforming the eastern Länder to a market-based economy; backward technology, shortage of investment over many, many years, and an ill-equipped labour-force, meant that much of the industrial structure was effectively obsolete.

The situation was of course unique in that West Germany stood ready, in effect, to underwrite the process of reform in the East — a luxury unavailable to the other reforming economies. An element of moral hazard inherent in that guarantee has already begun to show, however, with workers in the East, for example, pursuing much higher wages than current productivity levels can justify.

The former GDR was small compared with West Germany in terms of both population and economic activity, so unification might have been expected not to have any very significant ramifications for the world economy as a whole. The impact of unification has, however, turned out to be disproportionate, particularly for other ERM countries, because of the pressure placed on public finances and monetary policy in Germany. The budgetary cost of unification has strained Germany's public finances to the point where, even after restrictive measures announced in the budget, the public sector deficit is running at some 5% of GDP. Consequently, interest rates have had to remain higher than might otherwise have been the case, with implications for monetary conditions in the Community as a whole. And the uncertainty surrounding German prospects has undoubtedly been one of the key factors contributing to quite sharp movements in the DM (and other ERM currencies) against the dollar this year. Just the risk that the ERM anchor might drag creates a fresh and potentially unwelcome situation. The resolution of the Bundesbank is not in question, however, so the risks should turn out to be immaterial.

Nevertheless, the German experience of economic and monetary union in one country has provided a keen practical focus for the debate on EMU in the European Community. It highlights the risks of moving too quickly where there is no political imperative; and at a more detailed level it has given an important twist to the discussions on fiscal policy. On the one hand Germany's experience points to the desirability of achieving some degree of convergence amongst budgetary positions — and that must mean convergence on budgetary strength. On the other hand it demonstrates the practical difficulty of allowing for the unexpected.

The Gulf Crisis

No-one expected that the historic developments in Eastern Europe could be eclipsed by another world event, but for nearly a year events in the Gulf inevitably held centre stage. Although troubles in the region continue, we can now reasonably consider the economic implications. Some have even wondered why the conflict created concerns about the world economy. But memories are short. The fact of the matter is that, although world growth was already slowing a little by last summer, the slowdown became distinctly more pronounced following the invasion of Kuwait.

This was not a *direct* consequence of events in the Gulf themselves. The reason was rather the widespread depressant effect that the Gulf crisis had on business and consumer confidence throughout the world. Whilst this was most clearly visible in the case of travel and tourism, it operated across the whole spectrum of activity, reflecting three main concerns. *First,* that the loss of Iraqi and Kuwaiti oil production (around 4.5 mbd), coupled with the wider threat to supplies from the region, might drive prices to levels which would induce (as in 1979) a sharp international recession. In the event, while prices initially rose sharply they subsequently stabilised and then fell back to pre-crisis levels; those movements reflected the rapid offsetting increase in production by other OPEC countries, the extent and speed of which took many market observers by surprise. *Secondly,* there was initially a fear that the conflict might become a wider confrontation within the region. And *thirdly,* there was a concern that the freeze on the assets of Iraq and Kuwait, coupled with the substantial capital flight from the region in the immediate post-invasion period, might lead to financial problems and possibly even banking collapses in the region.

In this age of mass communications and instant opinion-making, a little jolt to confidence can go a long way. Both business behaviour and financial markets tend to respond with something of a herd instinct; not without some justification, as one man's postponed investment is another's lost order. In retrospect, however, the dent to confidence was not enormous and, with the war over, confidence has recovered, notably in the US.

8

The Gulf crisis has worsened the financial situation in that part of the world during a period when some progress has been made in resolving the wider problems of LDC debt and setting debtor countries on the road to recovery.

The so-called Baker Plan envisaged middle-income LDCs growing out of their debt problems, with the help of sound adjustment policies and new injections of funds from both the commercial banks and the international financial institutions (IFIs) — a term which covers the IMF, the World Bank and so on. The hope was that countries could consequently regain a more normal relationship with the international capital markets.

In the event the Baker Plan proved too optimistic about the growth potential of the countries concerned and banks were, understandably, reluctant to lend more money to countries which were not fully servicing existing debts. Thus in 1989 the so-called Brady initiative was launched. This went a step further in proposing that official funds from the IFIs should be available to support debt reductions by the banks, though still always conditional on sound adjustment policies. A number of debt reduction packages along these lines have been negotiated successfully over the past two years.

Meanwhile the *poorest* countries, mainly those in Africa, have benefited from official debt reduction through the Paris Club (which deals with government and other official sector claims). This has built on the "Toronto" initiative, and there is now a prospect of more generous relief once the terms of the British-inspired "Trinidad" initiative are settled. *In broad outline,* under the Toronto Terms some creditor countries agreed to cancel around one third of payments due, while others made a broadly equivalent reduction in the interest charged. These concessions were restricted to the poorest countries — those with a GNP per head of $580 or less — but the effects were modest because the relief applied only to payments as they became due. Under the UK's proposals, the whole stock of a country's debt would be tackled *at one go* and a proportion as high as two-thirds might be cancelled. Work continues on this.

The lower-middle-income debtor countries — which fall between the middle-income group, on which the Brady and Baker plans focused, and the poorest group in the Toronto/Trinidad category — present a special problem. The amounts at stake are in many cases very large and are mostly owed to official creditors, who have yet to be convinced that these countries lack the capacity — as distinct from the willingness — to service their debts in the long run. In two cases, however, the need for substantial write-downs of debt has been accepted by official creditors: the recent agreement for Poland provides substantial official debt relief, and Egypt may receive relief of a similar dimension. But the imperative of the case-by-case approach has been re-emphasised, and the treatment accorded to these two will not be readily extended to others.

While no one should be proud of the history of the LDC debt saga, some comfort can be derived from the manner in which the problem has been tackled over the past few years. A number of countries are, under IMF and IBRD auspices, tackling internal adjustment and economic reform. Some have been able to pass the key test of rehabilitation — a return to borrowing on normal terms as willing borrower from willing lenders. At the same time the banks have played a responsible and constructive role; by and large they have received fair value in debt reduction exercises or other voluntary exits, given the chances of eventual recovery if they were to hold on.

Financial Fragility

In the mid-1980s, Third World debt overhung the banking industry and created concerns of a crisis. Other concerns have taken over, however, with the current anxiety being "financial fragility", although it is often left rather vague whether this is meant to cover the banks themselves or their customers.

There is no doubt that many banks expanded their lending during the boom years of the late 1980s without adequate regard to the risks. As a result, while still recovering from the overdose of LDC debt, banks and other financial institutions in different countries became variously afflicted by junk bonds, over-exposure to real estate, falling stock markets and, most recently, the general onset of recession. It is a credit to the supervisory arrangements which are now in place that these various shocks have not had more profound effects on the world's banking system. This has been greatly helped by efforts over nearly a decade to strengthen banks' capital ratios; efforts that culminated in the Basle Convergence Agreement, which sets an international minimum standard.

Some have claimed that this has had a significant macro-economic effect, through a so-called credit-crunch. In fact, only in the US does there appear to be firm support for the view that some banks have been unusually cautious in their lending, to the point that it is reported that some creditworthy borrowers could not obtain more credit at any price. But even in the US it is hard to judge whether there has been anything of this sort on a significant scale; and still harder whether it is a true case of market failure, or simply the con-sequence of banks becoming more cautious on account of a deteriora-tion in the creditworthiness of potential customers brought about by the downturn itself. Furthermore, the structure of the US banking system has compounded — and partly been a source of — the problems there.

On balance, however, the difficulties of the banking industry *world-wide* have probably not had a significant macro-economic impact in global terms.

Uruguay Round

In the background, and less remarked on than the other developments covered here, is the Uruguay Round trade talks. The history of the post-war era confirms that liberal trading regimes promote growth, but also suggests that progress towards free trade on a truly global scale is achieved only through the painstaking multilateral negotiations of GATT Rounds, between which there are too often relapses into creep-ing protectionism. Failure in the talks is not, by its nature, something which could be expected to have a material effect in the near term; that could too easily lead to the talks finding a low place amongst international priorities. But in fact, a successful and substantive Uruguay Round is essential for the longer-term health of the world economy, and failure could have severe long-term consequences, not least for the developing countries. It is vital that every effort is made to ensure the talks succeed.

Macro-economic Outlook

The six developments described above — reform in the Eastern bloc, GEMU, the Gulf crisis, progress with LDC debt, financial fragility and the Uruguay Round — are illustrative of the changing and often unpredictable circumstances which confront the world economy. The immediate world economic outlook will be mainly dependent, however, on the resilience of the industrial countries in counteracting

11

recession and restoring sustainable growth, and above all in pursuing price stability.

The lesson of the past decade is that, if the world's leading economies persist with steady policies aimed at *non-inflationary* growth, they should, taking one year with the next, be successful in achieving broadly that. The danger in current circumstances, as in the past, is to give too great a stimulus and so spark off higher inflation (which could only be subsequently eliminated by policies which brake activity).

The consensus of forecasters is that, after having slowed to 2½% last year and perhaps less than 1% this year, growth of the industrial countries, which together account for the lion's share of world output, will be back at 2½% in 1992. The USSR and Eastern Europe are, however, likely to continue to move backwards for another year or so, with the longer-term outlook being particularly uncertain, notably for the Soviet Union, whose economic future must rest as much as anything on political developments there. The rest of the developing world as a whole may be expected to enjoy a period of moderate growth, although the pick-up may be delayed in those countries directly affected by the Gulf conflict.

In the longer term, global prosperity will be influenced by the success of reform and adjustment in Eastern Europe and the LDCs, and by the outcome of the Uruguay Round. It may also depend on the degrees to which the leading industrial countries succeed in co-operating to their mutual advantage in the exercise of economic policy. Co-operation, of the type practised in the G7 groups, has not perhaps received great acclamation, but in fact it has considerable achievements to its name, including averting clearly inconsistent policies, but more significantly in acting as a non-inflationary club.

It has been argued by some that such co-operation may be less easy in future. The argument is as follows. With the ending of the Cold War and the final and complete discredit of the archetypal centrally-directed economy, the tide of reform to market-based policies is surging around the globe, largely unresisted. But, it is argued, in the past security considerations, in the old East-West sense, had the effect of encouraging Western governments to hide their disagreements and pursue compromises on economic issues; these forces, it is suggested, are now much weaker, so that there will be starker confrontations and less co-operation on economic issues between the major economic powers — the US, Japan and Europe.

This casts central banks and governments in singularly blinkered roles. In practice, years of experience in these issues have, one would trust, made them conscious enough of the dangers of, for example, escalating protectionism and beggar-my-neighbour macro policies, so that such a deterioration in economic relations would be unlikely. While one cannot but be discomforted by the many calls to defend or extend protection that issue from various lobbies around the world, I am confident that they will not win the day.

2. Challenges facing Banks

A slightly different picture emerges if the developments described above and the current situation are looked at from the point of view of the banking industry. The prolonged period of growth since the early 1980s — reasonably steady and reasonably free of inflation — has not been a particularly steady period for the world's banking community, given LDC debt, the more recent problems associated with declining real estate and stock prices, and the introduction of more rigorous supervisory standards.

At the same time, deregulation has been sweeping through the financial services industry. The barriers to entry into particular activities or locations have been falling away. More is to come, as the EC completes its Single Market programme, and possibly as a result of structural reform in the US and Japan, although the outcome there is still far from clear. The Uruguay Round should, if successful, deliver further liberalisation.

Deregulation has opened up many new opportunities, but where there is an opportunity to make money there is also invariably a risk of losing it. Competition has been intense. In certain parts of the financial sector — securities business in London is an obvious example — new capacity was built up to a point where it seemed most unlikely that it could be fully utilised in normal market conditions; and so it has proved.

In these circumstances banks face a number of challenges. Most obvious is the need for a sound capital base. Inevitably, those who can raise capital most easily are often those who need it least, and conversely. But on the whole it will be no bad thing for individual banks to have to pause and make their existing capital work better, building up resources by the relatively slow process of retentions.

But what seems to have become as difficult as raising capital is identifying avenues for its profitable employment. Competition for low

13

risk business is so strong as to have forced margins to a bare minimum; and, in the eyes of some bankers, beneath the point of viability. There is, understandably, little enthusiasm to lend into developing countries or the emergent market economies of Eastern Europe, except where there is a clear sight of the cash flow required to service the debt, or some other form of security, or the prospect of a fruitful long-term relationship. Meanwhile, with the developed world growing only slowly at present — and some countries, including the UK, in actual recession — domestic opportunities for many of the world's major banks are by no means plentiful.

In the face of apparent over-supply and the pressures of competition, cost-cutting — or at least cost-containment — has become a central objective, together with a search for new sources of non-interest and fee income. There may therefore be some further retrenchment and consolidation. One possible response to the opening up of new markets would be more alliances and mergers rather than aggressive solo expansion; and this has already become evident within the European Community.

Some banks will, however, inevitably and rightly continue to seek new business through product innovation, and to exploit such niches as they may thereby create for themselves. But one lesson of the 1980s is that new products need to be tailored to identified customer needs if they are to make a durable impression.

But of all the available strategies, the one most often mentioned over the past year or so has been the return to "relationship" banking. Many banks appeared to lose their relationships during the 1980s. In part they were themselves responsible, as they switched their energies into new product areas or sought to pursue business selectively according to perceived short-term profits. In part the customers were also responsible, anxious to shop around for the cheapest service or source of funds in an intensely competitive marketplace.

The trend away from traditional banking relationships towards so-called transaction banking was particularly evident in the US and in this country. It was less so on the European Continent, where ties between bank and customer have historically been more complex — in some cases involving equity stakes — and hence more durable; and where securities markets were less well developed or more closely integrated with the banking industry itself.

Today banks are evidently keen to re-establish long-term relationships with selected customers, and in the present economic climate there are borrowers who may rue the fact that they turned away from long valued relationships during the boom. What is not clear is whether, given the highly competitive nature of the banking industry, strong enough relationships can be established to survive throughout the economic cycle. To achieve that, it seems that the relationship needs to be sufficiently close to enable the bank to anticipate and understand the customer's needs and problems.

The skill to service a relationship in this way is something which banks have been building up over a period of years, but a certain amount of damage was inflicted by the rush to "transaction" banking in the 1980s. For their part, customers would need to be open about their problems and be prepared to pay for a worthwhile relationship. Interestingly, there are signs that margins on corporate lending have been recovering in recent quarters from the excessively low levels previously reached. This is a healthy sign; it is certainly not, in this country, the symptom of a credit crunch.

Perhaps naturally enough there are sceptics who question whether the country has benefited from these years of deregulation and intensifying competition, and whether the UK was well-advised in leading the way. We were. The main beneficiaries have been the customers of financial services as a whole, who enjoy wider choice and more competitive prices. This will prove a potentially enormous benefit in the long term.

As to the banks themselves, they have had mixed experiences during the transition period when the various controls were relaxed or lifted. Mistakes have been made and lessons learned. But longer term benefits will come through. The conditions necessary for London to remain the pre-eminent financial centre in this time zone have been established. And it is certainly better to have led with reforms than to have waited and followed others.

3. Conclusion

In conclusion, banks face changes in both their macro and micro-economic environment. At the macro level, the economy of the developed world, though subject as ever to continuing surprises and shocks, seems reasonably well placed to shake off recession, with the monetary authorities determined to pursue price stability as the pre-condition for sustainable and steady growth. At the micro level, banks will continue to face the rapidly evolving competitive and techno-

15

logical environment. If there is a lesson to be drawn from the experience of recent years, it is perhaps the importance of taking the long view. Of course, it is not always possible to do so — few people would have predicted the changes that have occurred so rapidly in Eastern Europe for example, nor the pace of deregulation in some financial markets. But credit assessment is a field where more realistic risk analysis for the full life of a credit would in the past have rewarded such effort; and the revival of the notion of a long-term relationship with customers should benefit both banks and their customers.

Banks and Governments: Is Supervision needed in a Deregulated Economy?

Huib Muller
Chairman, Basle Committee on Banking Supervision

Huib Muller

Huib Muller was born in Indonesia in 1936 and educated at the Universities of Leiden and Michigan State.

In 1964 he joined De Nederlandsche Bank, becoming chief of the Credit System Supervision Department in 1968. He became an executive director in 1976 and had a special brief for (prudential) supervision of the credit system.

He was chairman of the EEC Banking Advisory Committee from 1982-85, having been a member of the Committee since 1977. In October 1988, he became chairman of the Basle Committee on Banking Supervision.

A Knight of the Order of the Netherlands Lion, Mr Muller was a speaker at the 1985 IBSS.

Contents

Huib Muller

Huib Muller died after a prolonged illness, before he could deliver this paper. He will be sadly missed all over the world.

He gave a paper at the 1985 School and had been particularly looking forward to coming to Cambridge again. He always believed that spreading information and understanding was vital to the development of world banking, and this paper is a fitting reminder of his own immense contribution.

Introduction

This paper argues that supervision of banks is a necessary burden if we are to enjoy the fruits of a deregulated financial system. Having examined the rationale for supervision in Section 1, it presents some observations on the present state of international banking in Section 2. Section 3 considers what supervisory standards are required in a deregulatory climate. The paper concludes by describing in Section 4 the topics that are on the Basle Committee's table for future policy convergence.

1. The Rationale for Banking Supervision

Banks are key institutions in the financial and economic health of our society. The truth of this statement does not need to be argued before an audience of bankers. However, it has become fashionable to question it elsewhere by reference to the proliferation of companies providing one or more of the services conventionally provided by banks. Many of these "non-banks" do in fact depend for their ultimate liquidity on the banking system and most observers find it difficult to deny the importance of banks at a time when the international press carries persistent reports (well-founded or not) of the damaging effect of a so-called credit crunch on the world's economy.

Notwithstanding the significance of banks, there are other important sectors in the economy which do not attract the attention of legislators and central bankers to the extent that banking does. Why are banks different? Why can the banking system not be left to market forces? Would this not improve efficiency by ensuring the survival of the fittest and the best? Why, on the other hand, do governments feel they must take steps to ensure that banks are prudently managed?

The traditional response is a familiar one to bankers. Because banks play a critical role in the payments system, and also hold the savings of the public, a wholly free market, in which entry to and exit from the industry is uncontrolled, creates the possibility of an unacceptable degree of risk. Market forces need, rather, to be tempered by criteria designed to ensure that only reputable banks are authorised, and by prudential standards designed to ensure that depositors are protected from excessive risk-taking.

Governments have a clear interest in promoting a strong and stable banking system, and this should be a priority, not only for domestic reasons, but also in international terms. The benefits accruing to a country which is successful in attaining those aims are

21

widely recognised. They cannot be achieved without an effective banking supervisory framework, so that the system's users have confidence that a strong banking infrastructure will be maintained in the future. Countries which fail to appreciate this at an early stage pay a penalty in a loss of confidence which is difficult to remedy. Governments in my experience do indeed recognise the contribution that sound, but sufficiently flexible, supervisory rules can play in this regard.

However, there are other, more fundamental, reasons for banking supervision. Banks by their nature transform maturities, ie they borrow short and lend long, naturally within prudent limits. This means that at any point in time a retail bank with a large core of demand deposits, however solvent on paper, would be unable to pay off all its liabilities as they mature. Instead it must rely on its depositors retaining a part at least of their balances. Depositor confidence is thus an essential ingredient for a stable banking system.

At present, most countries have deposit protection arrangements, which make bank "runs" by private depositors, like those of the 1930s, largely obsolete. On the other hand, growth in the interaction between financial market participants, through correspondent banking relationships, interbank lines, off-balance-sheet trading and many other forms of business, means that the failure of a bank can have widespread ramifications which may damage many more parties than was the case in earlier times. The bank "run" of the 1980s was a wholesale phenomenon, taking the form of a sudden drying-up of interbank funding, and a refusal by large creditors to roll over regular deposits leading to the danger of systemic disruptions in financial markets. In most countries, governments sought to prevent such events by being prepared to take action within an overall framework which could, but need not, involve official financial support, a policy described by President Corrigan of the Federal Reserve Bank of New York as having the attribute of "constructive ambiguity". Explicit and unambiguous safety net devices have risks of their own in terms of the weakening of market discipline on bank management to perform in a responsible manner and on bank shareholders and directors to hold management to high standards. They may also lead to the price of funding for certain banks being at a level, which may not truly reflect the risks involved. The burden then falls on supervision to compensate for the "moral hazard" created by a safety net which may appear over-generous. This does not, unfortunately, prevent the supervisor carrying the primary blame for a disaster in the eyes of the politicians, press and public, no matter how irresponsible the behaviour of the bank's management may have been.

The message I have to convey is that banking supervision on its own cannot be guaranteed to prevent banks from failing. Nor is it in the interests of bankers that it should, since this would mean much too great an involvement by the supervisor in the taking of banks' decisions, thereby stifling all initiative. It is my belief that market discipline, through judicious application of the *caveat emptor* principle, whereby depositors and creditors continue to exercise judgement in their dealings with banks, is the best means of ensuring the correct balance. To the extent that the safety net devices referred to above result in an oversupply of financial services, and thus to the weakening of standards, some measure of supervisory oversight in the form of adequate minimum standards is an essential back-up to restore checks and balances to the system. These standards include responsible and qualified management with adequate operating systems and controls and sufficient capital strength to support the risks being undertaken.

Banks have an advantage over other players in the market because of their ability to accept deposits from the general public. The quid pro quo is that they accept these minimum standards.

2. The Present State of International Banking

These are not easy times to be practising the profession of banking. As has happened in the past, and will continue to happen by virtue of the cyclical behaviour of our economies, the end of an upswing leaves banks with assets diminishing in quality as over-extended borrowers are squeezed between falling order books and rising interest rates. To some extent, I would argue that the pain being felt — and this is not by any means evenly spread, but seems to be concentrated in the English-speaking countries — is the more acute because of the relatively long period since we were last at this stage of the economic cycle. Bankers tend to have short memories and in the face of economic growth lose that precious virtue of scepticism.

Nonetheless, there are some features of the present situation which appear rather different and these may have been accentuated by the significant changes which have taken place in the banking industry over the past decade. Banking has become more international, more competitive and more innovative. Each of these features can be commended and, taken together, they have indisputably improved the standards of banking services provided to customers, both depositors and borrowers. The ability of corporate customers to obtain financing packages precisely suited to their needs, and the tailoring of services to personal customers, represent benefits to the community at large which cannot all be easily quantified, but clearly represent an addition to our well-being, if not to our income.

This has not, however, been achieved without some cost to the banks themselves. In the first place, while innovative techniques have yielded rewards to those who have developed them, they also have the capacity to produce some unwelcome surprises as well. There have been enormous investments in technology, but some of this money has clearly been poorly directed. The intensification of competition has meant that many of the previously "safe" sources of bank income have proved unreliable in conditions where foreign banks and non-bank lenders and providers of financial services have progressively encroached on what has hitherto been hallowed turf. To the extent that traditional banking cartels have been dismantled, and market entry requirements relaxed, the benefits are clearly apparent. But in some areas the cut-throat nature of the competition, together with an oversupply of financial services, have reduced banks' margins to such an extent that, as a supervisor, I doubt whether the remuneration adequately covers all the risks. Meanwhile, the cost structure has proved difficult to control, particularly for those banks with extensive branch networks or heavy investments in the securities business. As a result, profitability has come under pressure and, where this has coincided with a downturn in the business cycle such as we witnessed last year, the consequences have been grave. Indeed, 1990 has been one of the worst years I can remember for bank profitability, and this applies in virtually every major country.

As usual, when banking conditions become more difficult, there is a tendency to blame the supervisor. It is therefore worth taking a little time to consider whether supervision has contributed to the present environment. In particular, some commentators seem to suggest that it is the supervisors' fixation on the need for capital that is creating the problems in the industry, by generating conditions in which banks are no longer willing to lend, however creditworthy the borrower might appear to be. Much attention has been given to what is emotively called a credit "crunch". This means, as I understand it, that even sound borrowers find it difficult and expensive to obtain credit. It is certainly true that banks have rediscovered that ancient quality of scepticism, but I see little sign of good borrowers failing to find accommodation, albeit perhaps needing to accept less generous margins than before. Rather, I wonder whether, after a period in which supervisors were accused of being too soft in their approach, bankers are not all too ready to blame the Basle capital standards for refusing further credit to those whom they may have until recently been courting assiduously.

But what is this mysterious concept "capital" and why do the supervisors want to see more of it in the system? At its simplest, capital is the economic net worth of a bank, that is, the value of its assets less its liabilities. The critical word is "value". One of the principal responsibilities of bank supervisors is to ensure that banks value their assets at what they are worth to the bank. To a large extent, such valuations must rely very much on the judgement of the bank's management. The supervisor, supported by the auditor, can seek to ensure that the bank's procedures for assessing its credit portfolio are adequate, and that arrangements are in place for making provision against those assets that have deteriorated in value in a timely fashion (see the second paragraph of Section 4 for more on this). Sometimes the supervisor may believe that a particular bank is slow in making these value adjustments, or in adapting its provisioning policy to changes in the economic environment, and perhaps the bank may regard that opinion as excessively conservative. However, at a time when a number of countries are experiencing a cyclical downturn in their economies, where significant declines are taking place in the value of property and other pledged assets, and where there are well-publicised cases of borrowers experiencing problems in servicing their debt, it is hardly surprising that supervisors are concerned that banks take a critical look at their portfolios and make the necessary adjustments to the carrying value of their assets.

It is also no surprise, in this environment, that banks generally, and particularly in those countries where there have been particularly severe declines in asset values, should be taking a more cautious approach in extending credit. Clearly, the withdrawal symptoms are painful for those who have become used to easily available credit. A level of gearing that is high in historic terms has become common, not only among the more aggressive entrepreneurs, but also among households in many countries. As a result, the level of indebtedness is often such that "bailing out" these borrowers with further extensions of credit at high real interest rates is not necessarily the answer. Nor is it the right moment to relax supervisory standards: as I have said before, no one would dream of relaxing car safety standards in stormy weather. What we need now, in my view, is a somewhat less frenetic period, a calm between the storms, if you like, in which economic agents are allowed to adjust to a more realistic view of the future and the personal sector is allowed to rebuild its savings. I would not describe such a process as a credit crunch, but rather as a cleansing process which is necessary from time to time to permit bankers to get back to the fundamentals of banking and to enable customers to restructure their balance sheets. This process would have the welcome result of improving the quality of bank assets.

But there is a more basic structural problem. I believe that much of the world is presently over-banked. At the retail level the situation is perhaps worst in Europe with one branch for every 2,000 people. At the wholesale level, corporate customers are often inundated with offers of banking facilities by a plethora of banks offering very similar services. There is surely now a need to reduce excess capacity if long-run profitability is to be strengthened. This would not necessarily result in higher prices for banking services; in many cases the cost structure could be reduced by sensible rationalisation. In my own country the two largest banks, ABN and AMRO, have recently merged. Although some were surprised that the authorities allowed a move that might be seen as creating a dangerous monopoly, the Dutch banking market is now so open that we were confident that international competition would prevent our new banking monolith from abusing its position. On the contrary, we identified a substantial potential for cost savings that would enable the new bank to face the international market on a sufficiently strong footing to compete with the giants from France, Germany, Great Britain and elsewhere.

In any rationalisation process, the strong benefit and capital will clearly play a part here. The need for weak banks to shrink by withdrawing from unprofitable markets or by selling off marketable units gives those banks with spare resources an excellent opportunity. This is particularly noticeable in the United States where there has been distress selling of businesses and assets, especially those dependent on real estate values. This trend has also become evident in the emergence of "tiering" in the interbank market. While as a central banker with systemic responsibilities I do not necessarily welcome such tiering, I recognise it as a necessary part of the adjustment process in hastening rationalisation.

Another recent trend which supervisors will welcome is the recovery which has taken place in many countries in lending margins. Partly as a result of aggressive expansion by international banks over many years and the consequent oversupply of financial services, lending margins in international banking, in my opinion, fell to dangerously low levels. Now that some of the corporate borrowers which the banks supported so enthusiastically have experienced difficulties, it is clear that the spreads offered were much too thin to compensate for the credit risks incurred. It is also clear that banks took too little account of borrowers' overall indebtedness, partly as a result of the breakdown of what has now become known as "relationship banking" and partly through the growth of "deal" business. In some cases the consequent expansion of the number of banks involved with a single borrower led to serious underestimation of the borrower's total indebtedness. In a few countries, it is true, there is a reporting system for corporate indebtedness which enables a lender to check on a borrower's position, but in many of these systems borrowing from banks located in other countries escapes such reporting.

As I write, the prospects are for the banks' "core" lending business to become more profitable, reducing banks' dependence on the more transient sources of income such as fees, commissions and trading profits, and encouraging a belief that the levels of retained earnings will be able to recover, to the benefit of banks' capital resources. Risk awareness and the necessity to charge adequate risk premia have also been enhanced by the Basle capital framework, especially in so far as off-balance-sheet activities are concerned. However, in order that banks obtain the full benefit, dividend policy must not exert undue strains and a strict control needs to be kept on costs and risks. It will not be beneficial if wider spreads are merely a symptom of lower credit quality and result in an overall increase in loss experience. Recent signs also suggest that the capital markets may be recovering confidence. If bank managements can maintain the confidence of investors, and demonstrate a recovery in profitability and asset quality, external capital should be attracted back into the industry.

Summing up, therefore, while the present state of the international banking industry does give grounds for concern, I believe that pessimism is unjustified and that there will be a cyclical recovery. Nonetheless, it would be unrealistic to suggest that this can be achieved without any pain. As the British put it, "if it isn't hurting, it isn't working".

3. Supervisory Standards in a Deregulatory Climate

There is a common misconception that deregulation in some way implies a relaxation in supervisory standards. Although I do not propose to enter into semantics, my understanding of "deregulation" is that it means a removal of regulatory constraints, ie an increase in the scope of business that banks can do by relaxing or abandoning rules governing products, pricing or geography. While some commentators blame deregulation for the present ills in banking, I personally welcome it, as I am sure the members of the profession do. However, I would add one important rider, namely that deregulation clearly involves an increase in a bank's potential exposure to risk and must therefore be accompanied by an *increase*, not a decrease, in supervision. That is a quid pro quo about which some members of the profession might be more hesitant, but I believe most, on reflection, would accept it.

The United States has paid a fearful price for disregarding this precept, in the context of the Savings and Loans fiasco. Admittedly there are additional reasons, many of them a result of political factors, why the cost to the taxpayer became so enormous, but the origins of the story are clear. Briefly, rigid interest rate controls were maintained too long so that banks forgot to monitor their interest risk profile. Then these constraints were suddenly relaxed, with damaging consequences for institutions which had become over-accustomed to borrow short and lend long at managed rates; the situation was then compounded by allowing the institutions to enter into new areas of business without ensuring that they were properly qualified to assess the risks and without adequate supervision, but with the support of a very extensive public safety net in the form of a generous degree of deposit insurance.

How does supervision operate in a deregulated industry? The first point I would stress is that the supervisor should not seek to substitute *his* judgement for that of the bank. It is a banker's job to manage risk, particularly credit risk, which, dare I say it at this point of time, is the one with which he most has to contend. So I would dispel any fears (or hopes) you might have that the Committee I chair is about to produce a detailed blueprint of how bankers should manage risk.

However, the supervisor does have an important role to play in ensuring that banks have adequate systems to manage these risks and use those systems effectively. In today's world that is becoming an increasingly complex task. Judgement and perception of the risk are essential, leading to an understanding of a whole range of "worst case" scenarios. Where' possible, the supervisor likes to support his analysis of the quality of banks' risk management with some form of quantifiable minimum standard, however crude that may be. For example, derivative instruments were encompassed in the capital ratio exercise in a somewhat rough and ready manner.

An important element in risk management is what I have heard called "people risk". In most of the problem cases I have come across as a supervisor, the root of the problem has been bad management. By and large, good managements do not take on below quality assets or fail to ensure sound systems of internal control. The control systems needed to monitor risks on a continuous basis are of course costly, and very often the people who prevent banks from losing money do not receive as much reward as those who make it. But in my experience the former can contribute just as much to the viability of a bank over the long run. In today's volatile conditions the need for top management to allocate sufficient human resources to the internal control function cannot be emphasised too strongly. Supervisors can only encourage and check, they cannot devise the system. What they can do, however, and I believe this point is becoming increasingly accepted within the supervisory and banking communities, is to seek to ensure that the management of banks meet certain "fit and proper" tests.

Another concern of the supervisor in a deregulated environment is to see that capital standards are raised, since deregulation permits greater risk-taking and thus a greater potential for losses and a greater need for a safety cushion, enabling a bank to survive even when things go wrong. I am aware that there is a greater potential for profits too, but supervisors are by nature cautious, and their concern is ultimately for the users of the banking system and depositors in particular. Their interests are protected by seeing that the bank has adequate capital to cover the risk of loss.

As I mentioned in the previous section, the Basle Committee, which I have the privilege of chairing, has developed a minimum capital standard for application to international banks. This is not the place for a long explanation of the rationale lying behind this initiative, but I should record that it was the result of a clear perception by central bank Governors of the Group of Ten industrial countries that the capital strength of the international banking system needed to be

29

strengthened. Recognising that competitive pressures, made it very difficult for individual countries to increase their capital requirements unilaterally, and were in fact tending to lead to some "competition in laxity" in prudential standards, the Committee was asked to develop global standards for a global marketplace.

The result is of course a series of compromises which do not wholly satisfy any party to the agreement, but which each is prepared to live with in the interests of the common goal. Banks themselves welcomed the capital standards at the time, although I suspect some wished that they had taken the trouble to position themselves a little more carefully when market circumstances were more favourable. All banks, I believe, welcome the principle of the level playing-field, even though that cannot be achieved by capital standards alone, however evenly applied. And many banks, though they did not necessarily do so initially, will now recognise that the central-bank Governors were quite right to call for an increase in the capital in the system at the time they did.

Another purpose of the Basle capital standards was to address the rapid growth in off-balance-sheet risks, many of which resulted from the innovations introduced in the 1980s. While the new requirements have not by any means brought the growth of the derivative markets to a halt — and this was not of course an objective — the credit risks arising in these markets are at least being captured for capital measurement purposes, and this allows supervisors and perhaps even some senior bankers to sleep more easily.

The purpose of the Basle capital accord, in summary, is therefore to raise the minimum level of capital (I would stress the word "minimum", because for many banks and banking systems I would regard the 8% standard as far too low); to remove some of the unevenness in the playing-field for international banks; and to capture risks which were escaping measurement in existing national systems by being booked off the balance sheet.

A final judgement on the impact of this agreement, which is still in its transitional phase, is clearly premature, and it may be some time before the full effects have worked through. Initial reactions, however, suggest that the accord is exerting a healthy discipline on the behaviour of banks. They are now looking hard at the capital cost of their activities in terms of perceived risk. While I would caution against overdue regard for the weights used, which are meant to be broadbrush in their impact and not to substitute for reasoned credit analysis, I would judge that the concentration on capital cost brings efficiency benefits and helps banks to price their products economically. I accept that those borrowers who perceive themselves as suffering from weightings which they might regard as discriminating may not welcome this feature, but my own experience is that sound borrowers continue to obtain funds at keen rates. I have not heard complaints from the Royal Dutch/Shell group or from IBM about the 100% weight such companies attract.

Perhaps one or two figures on the direct capital costs of an 8% solvency requirement might be of interest. Assume, for example, that the standard interest rate on borrowed funds is 6%; that core capital comprises two thirds of total capital and subordinated debt the remaining one third; that the subordinated debt carries an 6.5% interest rate; and that the target *gross* return on core capital is 18.5% (ie a 12.5% net return assuming a 33% tax rate). In these circumstances, the required net interest margin needed to generate the required returns on debt and equity would be 68 basis points[1]. Of course, this calculation refers only to the cost of capital itself and does not take account of overheads, default risks and other elements which a bank would wish its margins to cover.

An important aspect of the agreement which caused some concern when it was first formulated was that banks' competitive positions would suffer in comparison with other competing institutions. The Committee took a fairly robust view on this matter, arguing that banks had an advantage over other players in their ability to accept deposits from the general public. It was therefore reasonable that they should expect a heavier supervisory burden.

Nonetheless, the Basle Committee continues to pursue the ideal of developing global standards which apply across the different supervised sectors. The Committee has been working in close collaboration with securities regulators in order to try to ensure that all participants in the securities markets, both bank and non-bank, compete on an equivalent footing. This has meant some fundamental rethinking of the supervisory treatment of position risk, in order to come closer to the techniques currently used by securities regulators.

---

1   The algebra works as follows:
$\frac{2}{3}$ x 8% x (18.5% – 6%) + $\frac{1}{3}$ x 8% x (6.5% – 6%) = 0.68% or 68 basis points. If a bank had a higher target capital ratio, say 10%, the required margin would rise to 85 basis points, again assuming the same scenario for funding costs. So it can be seen that a 1% margin could easily result.

More recently, a dialogue has been initiated between banking and insurance regulators. Here, too, it may be possible in due course to consider some convergence in the approach to risk measurement between the two sets of regulators. At this juncture, however, it is fair to say that there are marked differences in the philosophy lying behind the capital adequacy requirements of banking and insurance regulators. In particular, whereas bank supervisors are mainly concerned with assessing risk in the assets of a bank, insurance regulators also need to concern themselves with risks on the liabilities side of the balance sheet.

4. The Future of Convergence

In conclusion, this paper describes what the Basle Committee is doing to further the process of co-operative development of banking supervision throughout the world. The Committee continues to give considerable importance to the need to maintain and improve standards of capital adequacy. The 1988 agreement needs time to be fully implemented — the transitional period will be completed by the end of next year — and its effects assessed. No doubt it will then need to be reviewed, and the possibility of some modifications in the light of experience cannot be ruled out. However, aware as they are that the 8% ratio may in many cases provide inadequate protection, supervisors are more likely to favour a tightening of the rules than a relaxation.

There are, however, a number of areas referred to in the agreement itself where more work needs to be done to complete the framework. A first step was a review of the inclusion in capital of general reserves or provisions for bad and doubtful debts. Proposals have recently been made which will make clear that amounts set aside in respect of a perceived deterioration in a group of assets, such as exposures to heavily indebted countries, even if not allocated to specific loans, should not be included in capital. Another area relates to the treatment of what have become known as market risks, that is to say the risk of loss arising out of positions in foreign exchange, traded securities and exposure to interest rate risk. This is an exceedingly complex area, but there are some guiding principles which the Committee is following. The first is to develop measurement systems which are as simple as possible but adequate to track the actual risks. The second is that these systems should be capable of application by the banks, including those that will have a need to develop more sophisticated approaches for their own management purposes. The third is that the approach should be capable of being applied to all international banks no matter from which country they come. These basic principles prove a formidable challenge, but the Committee believes it is well on the road to producing supervisory tools that will meet them. However, none of these will be imposed on the industry without a due process of consultation and testing.

On foreign exchange we have made good progress, although we are sometimes accused of too much simplicity. It is difficult, for example, to take into account cross-positions in different currencies with different volatilities in their mutual relationships without sophisticated statistical techniques. The supervisor would need to play a more prominent role in specifying risk parameters than he would wish to do. A simple capital requirement on overall open positions is the likely outcome. On position risk in traded securities we have the added problem that it is necessary to agree a basis of approach with the regulators of non-bank securities houses that are in direct competition with banks in this business. As mentioned earlier, the need for co-ordination with securities regulators is now widely accepted, and the basic building-blocks are in the process of construction. An essential element is that the risk on positions in debt securities, in large part a form of interest rate risk, should be capable of incorporation in an overall measure of interest risk in all of the bank's operations. This last area is the most difficult but probably also the most important. There are differences of opinion, not just among supervisors, but also among those banks with which concepts have been tested. A considerable period of experimentation and analysis is likely to be needed before an appropriate capital requirement can be drawn up for this element of market risk.

A further area of interest concerns the supervision of liquidity. Discussion of this issue has inevitably reflected the major differences that exist in the way national systems are structured, and also the ambiguity that exists in arrangements designed for the prudential supervision of individual banks and those that exist to ensure the stability of markets and facilitate the operation of monetary policy. Nonetheless, progress is being made in identifying common ground in member countries' arrangements for the supervision of liquidity. It is intended in due course to produce a paper designed to help supervisory authorities clarify their objectives and provide a basis for establishing a satisfactory policy for the prudential supervision of liquidity, and if possible to identify some form of standard by which liquidity can be judged. The difficulty is to gauge the relative importance of traditional quantitative tests, which rely on a number of behavioural assumptions about issuers and holders, and more judgmental assessments which need to be capable of objective measurement.

A relatively new topic that is concerning bank supervisors is the supervision of financial groups that include other non-bank financial intermediaries. The growth of financial conglomerates is proceeding apace in those countries where it is permitted, and legal barriers preventing such groups in other jurisdictions seem likely to disappear in the foreseeable future. The problems are more readily dealt with where the parent company is a bank supervised by an authority with power to supervise on a consolidate basis. More difficult are cases where the parent is another institution, either regulated by an authority without such powers, or not regulated at all. There are no easy answers to these questions, in part because all financial conglomerates are different, but banking, securities and insurance regulators are now attempting to devise some common principles or understandings to guide them in their task and to provide a structure for the necessary degree of inter-authority co-operation.

There is little doubt that whether we like it or not — and we *should* like it — the process of deregulation will continue. It is also clear that the extent and nature of the risks incurred by banks demand a greater degree of supervision on a highly professional basis. Despite the dangers ahead, both during the current downturn and in the longer perspective, I have no doubt that banks will survive and prosper within the context of flexible yet firm and consistent supervision.

Dynamics of Competition in Banking

Ian Morison, FCIB
*Midland Group Professor
of Banking and Finance
Loughborough University*

Professor Ian Morison, FCIB

Born in 1945 and educated at Collyer's School, Horsham and Lincoln College, Oxford, he joined *The Times* in 1966 as a financial journalist, becoming its banking correspondent and deputy financial editor.

In 1974 he moved to the Inter-Bank Research Organisation, heading its public policy group until 1980, when he was appointed head of public affairs to the Committee of London Clearing Bankers. Between 1983 and 1988 he was assistant general manager and corporate affairs director at Midland Bank, with responsibility for strategic planning and external relations.

Ian Morison was appointed Midland Group Professor of Banking and Finance at Loughborough University in December 1988 and Director of the university's Banking Centre the following year.

He has written and lectured extensively in banking and related topics. He delivered the 1980 and 1981 Gilbart Lectures on banking at the University of London, and presented papers to the 1981 and 1989 Cambridge Seminars of The Chartered Institute of Bankers.

Contents

Introduction

It is a cliche of our time that competition in the banking industry has increased massively in the United Kingdom and world-wide over the past decade or two. Deregulation and technological change are seen as the main causes of competitive change, and its consequences are usually assumed to be benign for the users of banking services, though not of course for all of the traditional providers. This paper sets out to explore some of the more important causes and consequences of competitive change in banking, with examples drawn in the main from the UK experience.

The paper starts by considering the nature of competition and in particular the recent shift of academic emphasis from purely static assessments of the state of competition within an industry to more dynamic considerations of market structure, conduct and performance. It then considers the nature of the banking industry, emphasising the increasing importance of non-banks as competitors in parts of that industry. The paper next describes some of the salient features of the highly uncompetitive banking markets of the fairly recent past, noting, not only their inefficiencies, but also their more benign features of predictability and cohesion.

The central section of the paper considers the causes of competitive change, and argues that the most important engines of change are to be found in the basic cost structure of the industry. This argument is supported by evidence drawn from different functional cost areas, including technology and marketing.

Finally, the paper considers some of the key consequences of increased competition — on the range of services that banks provide, on pricing policy, on the extent of diversification, on the development of new financial markets and on the "bundling" of financial services. Although in certain respects the immediate consequences of increased competition have involved considerable market turbulence, this largely reflects the fact that competitive forces were dammed up for too long and is not a justification for turning the clock back on deregulation.

1. The Nature of Competition

It is right to start by asking what we mean when we say that banking has become more competitive. One thing which we do not necessarily mean is that there are more banks now than there were, say, 10 or 20 years ago. On the contrary, in many countries the number of banks and kindred institutions has declined significantly as a result of takeovers and mergers. In some countries, it was the very existence of uncompetitive market conditions which permitted large numbers of banking institutions to survive — US banks and UK building societies being two obvious examples. In both cases, as conditions have become more competitive, so the number of institutions has declined.

This point is worth stressing, if only because of the tendency, reinforced by basic economic textbooks, to assume that the state of competition in an industry correlates neatly with the number of firms in that industry. To assume that industries with a large number of firms are, *ipso facto*, competitive while those with a small number are uncompetitive is a fallacy which could give rise to expensive errors of public policy, such as the official sponsoring of new banks for which there might be no real market need, or the placing of unnecessary anti-trust obstacles in the way of mergers between existing ones.

Economists working in the area of competition theory and policy have attempted to take account of the limitations of the static model by developing two concepts which are both of help in providing insights into the current state of competition in the banking industry.

The first is the concept of "workable" or "effective" competition[1], which combines both static (structural) and dynamic aspects of competition in order to see how, in the imperfect real world, competitiveness may best be assessed and promoted. The state of competition in an industry will typically be considered under the three complementary headings of structure, conduct and performance, with importance attached to assessments of relative as well as absolute competitiveness.

The second is the concept of contestable markets[2] which, as the name suggests, focuses less on the existing number of firms in an industry than on the presence or otherwise of entry (and exit) barriers to that industry: the fewer the barriers, the more contestable the market. A totally contestable market, albeit one with a limited number of firms producing varied products, would generate the same benefits in terms of economic welfare as the textbook case of the perfectly competitive market of many firms where each has to accept the market price and the product is homogeneous.

The main implication of these theoretical developments for this paper is that it will be concerned less with the raw number of competitors in the banking industry than with the other factors which condition their behaviour — in particular, changes in cost factors, though changes in the relative market power of banks and their customers, and changes in the legal and regulatory environment in which banks operate, are also important.

If the word "competitiveness" is less straightforward than it may at first appear, the same is also notoriously true of the word "banking". A banker, as Lord Denning pointed out in a memorable judgment in 1966, is easier to recognise than to define. Any attempt to assess the competitiveness of an industry is liable to be bedevilled by problems of defining the boundaries of that industry; but these problems are particularly acute in the case of banking.

The services of financial intermediation that banks provide can be broken down in numerous ways — by customer type, by geographic market, by functional specification — and in their deconstructed form most of these services are also provided, in one configuration or another, by non-banks. Firms tend to be called banks when they provide a particular configuration of financial services; but it would clearly be wrong to restrict an assessment of the state of competition in banking to banks. Other firms — near-banks, non-bank financial institutions and industrial and commercial companies alike — are also actual and potential participants in different parts of the banking market and must be taken into account.

Whether or not the number of fully-fledged banks has increased in any given country, there can be little doubt that the number of participants in particular parts of the banking market has. This reflects both diversification by established banks — from retail into investment banking, for example — and the increasing provision of banking services by non-banks, facilitated by deregulation and technological change. Not only has the number of actual competitors in particular parts of the market increased, but the entry barriers faced by potential competitors have been lowered, which has also had a major impact on contestability and hence on competitive behaviour.

Last but not least, market power has shifted perceptibly and almost certainly irreversibly from banks to their customers as banks have lost some of the advantages of superior information and reputation which they traditionally enjoyed over non-banks and capital markets. This shift has been particularly evident in the United States, where demanding disclosure requirements make it easy for ultimate investors to assess corporate risk before investing directly in bonds and commercial paper. In countries like Germany and Japan, by contrast, the power of banks is still largely buttressed by the privileged

41

information they hold about their customers[3].

2. Banking in Uncompetitive Times

Before analysing the effects of increased competition in banking, it may be helpful to consider, as a point of reference, what a thoroughly uncompetitive banking system might look like. Fortunately, this is not too difficult an exercise: one merely has to remember what most national banking systems did look like in the 1960s or even, in many instances and respects, through the 1970s and early 1980s.

Take British banking prior to the reforms of 1971, for example. A combination of formal rules, informal suasion, collusive agreements and lack of zeal ensured that there was little if any competition in the volume of business undertaken; in the interest rates charged and paid to customers; in the variety of deposit and loan facilities available to customers; in the willingness of bankers to test the frontiers of risk; in their propensity to develop ancillary products, or in such important attributes of quality of service as branch opening hours.

Some of the more important consequences of this lack of competition are worth recalling. With interest rates almost always held below the market clearing level, various forms of non-price rationing had to be invoked. Since banks were able to lend all they were allowed to, at reasonable margins, to customers of demonstrable credit-worthiness, they rationed to a large extent by perceived quality. The loans they extended were typically repayable on demand, secured, and directed at well-established businesses. Newly-established firms and private individuals received short shrift, while term loans to finance industrial investment were almost unheard of. In short, the banks — just like any monopolist in an economics textbook — withheld output from the market.

At the same time, building societies were operating rationing systems of a rather different nature — giving priority to existing savers, operating mortgage queues, or lending lower multiples of salary or lower percentages of valuation than could be justified on prudential grounds alone. The interest rate structure was operated by a Building Societies Association Council, which was dominated by medium-sized societies with relatively high administrative costs to recover, and it therefore guaranteed generous margins for the more efficient large societies which could use the proceeds to finance ambitious branch expansion programmes.

These are just a few examples — many more could be cited — of ways in which major competitive imperfections in the banking market resulted in asset and liability portfolio structures and income and expense flows which were different in both quantitative and qualitative respects from those which would have obtained in the absence of those imperfections. One consequence was the form of managerial behaviour known as expenses preference whereby the economic rents that the lack of competition permitted ended up, not in the hands of the shareholders or the workers, but being expended on activities ranging from branch expansion to company car schemes, which reflected the personal aspirations of the managements of the institutions concerned.

A rather different consequence was a high degree of cross-subsidisation between different parts of the banks' business. Regardless of whether the banks' profits in aggregate were below or above an economically "normal" level, there is no doubt that some activities were markedly more profitable than others. Notoriously, the banks made high profits on the back of their personal customers, or more specifically those with relatively high balances and low activity levels on their accounts, and used these to subsidise their corporate and institutional lending business.

It is no coincidence that the personal customers concerned were, as a group, relatively price-insensitive: that is to say, they were unlikely to alter their banking habits as a result of changes in the interest rate and tariff structure facing them. With established banks scarcely competing amongst themselves, and with high entry barriers facing potential competitors, the excess profits earned on such business were not competed away.

Economists dislike uncompetitive market structures for three reasons. Producers do not expand output to the point where the marginal costs of production equate with the marginal benefits of consumption; monopoly pricing transforms a consumer surplus into a producer surplus; and the lack of competition engenders X-inefficiency — essentially a higher cost structure than would prevail in competitive conditions. The imperfect banking markets of the recent past undoubtedly displayed all three attributes to a greater or lesser extent.

3. The Benefits of Uncompetitive Banking

It cannot, however, be concluded from the previous section that unfettered competition in banking would be an unqualified desideratum. For a start, in banking as in any other industry, *all* the conditions for perfect competition have to be met for an optimal outcome in welfare terms to be guaranteed. In the real world this can clearly never be the case; and if the "first-best" outcome is unattainable, competitive imperfections may need to be tolerated in order for the "second-best" to be attained instead. More specifically, attempts to foster unfettered competition in banking could well have consequences even less palatable than the costs of imperfect competition illustrated above.

We shall be considering shortly what some of the unwonted consequences of financial deregulation have actually been. Here it is enough to recall that the previous lack of competition imparted a certain degree of predictability to the workings of the financial system; and predictable behaviour (for instance, predictable holdings of liquid assets and predictable loan-to-deposit ratios) by financial institutions and markets is a condition of effective monetary and credit control policies.

Of course, the official regulations and controls of the past often gave rise to unintended, unforeseen and unwelcome side-effects, not the least of which was the emergence of under-regulated secondary banking markets; but these were rarely on the same scale as, say, the catastrophic response of the US savings and loans institutions to deregulation or the explosion in UK consumer and mortgage lending in the late 1980s. Competition — particularly in its more dynamic manifestations — almost inevitably involves unpredicted behaviour by market participants, so it is small wonder that regulators, with their vested interest in predictability, have at best an ambivalent attitude towards the enhancement of competition in banking. It can be demonstrated that a system in which the monetary authorities directly influence the amount and direction of credit is inherently stabler than one in which the process is left to market forces; the more competitive a banking system is allowed to become, therefore, the greater the need for prudential regulation.

Nor should it be assumed that collusive behaviour between financial institutions is always a bad thing. A banking system in which the public enjoys confidence has many of the properties of a public good, and gives rise to economic benefits which are external to the immediate providers and consumers of banking services. Thus there is a classic economic case for the state to intervene in the market mechanism to help ensure the necessary degree of public confidence. Nor does the argument stop there.

Part of that intervention may well involve persuading individual banks to act in consort — to support a company or another bank which may be undergoing severe liquidity problems, for example. The more competitive the banking market, the more likely a rational banker is to refuse to participate in any such proposed action, on the grounds that the benefits will accrue to the system as a whole rather than to his bank in particular: he will therefore seek to be a "free-rider" if a rescue is being mounted, bearing none of the costs but enjoying all of the general benefits.

As long as the Governor of the Bank of England could summon all the players in the banking game into the same parlour, moral suasion worked well enough at overcoming this sort of unenlightened self-interest during episodes such as the secondary banking crisis of 1974. Increased competition means that the conditions for effective suasion of this kind no longer exist, as the recent failure of the Bank to mount a successful rescue operation for British & Commonwealth Merchant Bank showed.

In short, while the banking markets of the recent past manifested all the kinds of allocative and operational inefficiency that economists would expect to see in the absence of effective competition, they also manifested a degree of predictability and cohesion in their behaviour which was not entirely without value. While few would wish to turn the clock back to the bad old days of almost totally uncompetitive banking markets, a price has inevitably to be paid for the benefits of greater competition. We shall return to this theme before the end of the paper.

4. Competition and Costs

Before considering the consequences of increased competition more closely, some further observations about the causes may be relevant. The state of competitiveness of an industry is a function, more than anything else, of its cost structure. High fixed costs mean that economies of scale can continue to be enjoyed by those firms large enough to attain high levels of output relative to the size of the industry as a whole. Such industries will tend to be dominated by a single monopolistic producer or a few oligopolists, since only they will be large enough to reap the advantages of low average costs. Small firms will become uneconomic, and will fail, be acquired or otherwise leave the industry. The high fixed costs will at the same time represent an entry barrier for any potential competitor to surmount; the fact that many of those costs will take the form of irrecoverable sunk costs represents an exit barrier which will further deter potential competitors, since even if they believe that profitable business opportunities do exist, they will be unable to exploit them by indulging in a "hit and run" strategy.

Where does the banking industry fit into this basic analytical framework? Until relatively recently, it would have been natural to emphasise the importance of fixed costs and scale economies, particularly in the field of retail banking where a strong capital base, extensive branch networks and large-scale data processing systems were of particular importance. The history of retail banking in most developed countries apart from the United States has, until recently, been one of consolidation of market power. In England and Wales, the hundreds of branch banks in existence in the early 19th century had been reduced by amalgamation and acquisition to a score or so by the early 20th, with a mere 11 members of the Bankers' Clearing House being reduced to just six by the mergers of the late 1960s. Similar stories of consolidation can be told in other countries, and in certain cases are still unfolding: witness the recent round of Nordic bank mergers and the union of AMRO and Algemene Bank Nederland. In some countries such as Italy mergers are indeed now being officially promoted in order to improve the banking system's international competitiveness.

Ironically, the relatively low number of prominent retail banks in most developed countries makes it very difficult to reach reliable conclusions about industry cost structures: it is really only in the United States, where custom and regulation have preserved over 13,000 separate commercial banks, that the empirical evidence is at all robust. It seems that the cost curve of a typical US bank is U-shaped, as opposed to being L-shaped or continuously declining. In other words, the advantages of scale economies may be reaped for a while, but will eventually be offset by higher input costs or managerial diseconomies.

While empirical evidence elsewhere may be poor, there are a priori grounds for believing that U-shaped cost curves may be the norm outside the United States as well as inside[4]. For instance, it can be shown that, while a medium-sized bank may enjoy significant advantages in terms of risk diversification over a small bank, the additional advantages available to a large bank are far less significant. To take another example, the arrival on the marketplace of many forms of third party supplier means that it is no longer necessary to be a large bank in order to enjoy the advantages of large clearing or processing systems.

Thus, economies of scale may be less potent than they used to be. At the very least, bank managements will have to work increasingly hard to identify and exploit them — though the opportunities that a bank merger could now provide to eliminate redundant activities and thus reduce the combined firm's overall cost structure could be considerable.

It is, inevitably, hard to analyse the diseconomies of scale that may help to account for a U-shaped banking cost curve. What is undoubtedly relevant, however, is that the business of banking is largely about the effective management of internal information flows, and the difficulty of this task increases with the size and complexity of the organisation. Large banks are also more likely to demonstrate managerial expenses preference. They are more vulnerable than small ones to adverse shifts in public and political opinion, and therefore may have to devote a higher proportion of their resources to managing external relationships.

5. The Growth of Selective Competition

The tentative conclusion at this stage must be that the cost structure of the banking industry does not seem to represent as high an entry barrier as it once did. This conclusion seems the more robust if one considers, not the banking industry as a whole (assuming this term has any real meaning nowadays), but any one of its separately contestable component parts. The fixed costs, and more especially the sunk costs, of establishing a bank *de novo* may still be prohibitive; but the fixed costs of competing in a particular niche of the banking market could well be much lower, both in absolute terms and as a proportion of total costs.

In this context the most important trend of recent years has been the deconstruction of hitherto integrated financial activities into their component parts. There is no longer a single activity called "lending", but a series of discrete functions — broking and initiation, administration, financing and asset-holding — which can be and increasingly are performed by separate agents. Deregulation, technology and financial innovation have encouraged or obliged participants in the banking market to concentrate on those particular functions where they enjoy competitive advantage, rather than following the "all or nothing" approach of the past.

Let us illustrate this point with just one example. Suppose a medium-sized building society wished to enter the consumer credit market. At first it might feel inhibited by the need to devote significant fixed costs, and sunk costs, to the development of the necessary administrative systems. But then it would realise that it could readily sub-contract the administrative function to a specialist instalment credit finance house. Its own role would be to initiate (market and sell) the loans and carry them on its balance sheet, for both of which activities the fixed costs would probably be very much lower.

Thus it is the cost structure, not of the business of banking as a whole, but of its myriad component parts that will increasingly determine the state of competition in the industry. This is the economics of cherry-picking. Institutions — whether domestic or foreign, financial or non-financial — will be able to decide in which particular part or parts of a banking market they wish to compete. Data processors, retailers, foreign banks, building societies and many other types of business are now making such decisions on a daily basis.

6. Cyclical versus Structural Trends

The key assumption here is that selective incursions into the banking market will represent a viable strategy for a significant number of competitors. Not so long ago, such an assumption would have been seriously questioned. Established banks, it would have been argued, enjoyed major advantages in terms of official status, market reputation, customer relationships, technical competence, capital strength and, not least, the quantity and quality of their internal information, which would serve to marginalise effective competition from outside their ranks. Put another way, established banks enjoyed absolute cost advantages and economies of scope which were not available to niche competitors.

This counter-argument still has some force. The recent sharp increase in selective competition has occurred at a time of unprecedented expansion in the demand for financial services, when novelty of approach and speed of response to emerging market needs have made it relatively easy for nimble competitors to attack the entrenched banks. The ability of newcomers to sustain that challenge when the economy as a whole is in recession and the financial services market is particularly depressed is now being tested. Two examples will serve to show how severe that test is proving.

Japanese and other foreign banks, having built up a substantial share of the UK corporate lending market during the 1980s, are now suffering disproportionately from the problems of the recession, and are often proving less able than the indigenous clearing banks to support ailing UK companies as those problems intensify. Wholesale mortgage lenders, who acquired a substantial share of the UK mortgage market in the late 1980s, despite the absence of a domestic deposit base or network of retail outlets, are now finding that the profitability of their business is particularly sensitive to the state of the interest rate cycle.

What this means is that some at least of the intensified competition in the financial services market in recent years has been cyclical rather than secular in nature. But while there may be some comfort here for the traditional banks, that comfort is strictly limited. For if one looks below the surface of the immediate competitive forces, there is no shortage of longer-term influences at work weakening the relative position of traditional banks and strengthening that of selective competitors.

Some of these influences have been at work now for a considerable time. For instance, the emergence in the 1960s of efficient secondary money markets allowed institutions of sufficient repute, such as foreign banks, to expand their lending activities without first having to invest heavily in deposit-gathering branch networks. More recently, the emergence of efficient markets in securitised debt instruments has improved access to the corporate lending market, both for banks able to initiate a corporate loan, but without the balance sheet capacity to hold that loan on their books, and for non-banks willing to hold such paper but lacking an existing relationship with the borrower.

7. Some Specific Entry Barriers

Technological developments are frequently cited as having lowered entry barriers to the banking industry, and there are certainly plenty of examples to support this assertion. An obvious one is the way in which developments in the technology of plastic cards, point-of-sale

49

terminals and telecommunications have facilitated the access of retailers to the payments and consumer credit markets. Another example would be the development of treasury management systems, which have allowed major corporate treasurers' departments, not only to economise in their use of traditional banking services, but also to offer cash management services to third parties.

Yet technological developments are creating new entry barriers as well as dismantling old ones. The level of commitment to systems expenditure that is now required in order to be an efficient and innovative competitor in the banking market is increasingly proving beyond the financial means of smaller firms. In these circumstances they may have to choose between leaving the market (which in effect means being acquired by a larger financial institution — the choice which many smaller building societies have been making) or contracting out their systems-intensive activities to third parties (an approach now being adopted by many small US banks).

Conflicting evidence is also apparent when one considers the importance of marketing expenditure as an entry barrier. Retail banks traditionally acquired most of their customers through a mixture of convenient branch location and word-of-mouth recommendation; thereafter, the provision of a simple range of near-identical banking products to a captive clientele hardly required great marketing effort. The position today is of course radically different.

A shift from relationship to transaction banking, the greater range and complexity of available financial products, and, of course, the intensification of competition itself have all required market participants to devote increasing resources to product research, development, promotion and delivery. As with technology, the level of necessary expenditure is increasingly beyond the means of smaller firms but not, of course, beyond the means of major foreign banks, retailers or other unconventional competitors. In this situation it is tempting for established banks to seek to emulate the fast-moving consumer goods industry and invest heavily in the creation of brand values; however, the commodity nature of most banking products is bound to limit the effectiveness of such a strategy.

In this review of entry barriers there remains the special case of authorisation and regulation. To engage in some of their activities, notably deposit-taking, firms in all developed countries have to demonstrate a certain minimum level of capital strength and technical competence. These requirements have become more explicit and more onerous in recent years. On the other hand, they are now being applied in a more even-handed way than heretofore, as a result of international harmonisation under the aegis of the Bank for International Settlements. So while the need for authorisation remains an important entry barrier, it is one which can now be more easily surmounted by institutions of a certain size and repute — notably, foreign banks attempting to enter a hitherto protected domestic banking market[5].

To summarise so far: the state of competition in an industry is largely determined by its cost structure, and in particular by the cost barriers facing new entrants; developments in the economics of the banking industry have lowered some though by no means all of these barriers; in some cases these trends have disadvantaged small existing participants while assisting non-traditional competitors; although entry barriers to the banking industry as a whole remain high, those to particular parts of the industry have fallen quite sharply; the resulting intensification of competition has been facilitated by buoyant demand and may be partially unwound now that market conditions are depressed; in these circumstances the established banks' advantages of economies of scope may reassert themselves; but, after allowing for cyclical factors, it is likely that much of the increased competitiveness of the banking markets will prove irreversible.

8. Six Consequences of Competition

Allowing then that the underlying economics of the banking industry have changed in recent years to facilitate greater competition, how has that competition manifested itself and what have been its main consequences? Partial answers to these questions have already been offered. For instance, the deconstruction of the banking market into its separately contestable parts is not only a cause of greater competition, by lowering entry barriers, but also a consequence: greater competitive rivalry will inevitably lead participants to search out those segments of the marketplace where they reckon they will enjoy competitive advantage.

A systematic assessment of the state of competition in banking would need to consider the subject under the three headings of structure, conduct and performance. At the structural level we would expect to see greater competitiveness reflected in an increased number of actual and potential competitors and lower concentration ratios.

Competitive conduct would be evidenced by the intensity with which participants strove with each other to identify and meet market needs. The financial performance of a competitive industry would be characterised by profits which, over time, were neither abnormally high nor abnormally low.

For the purposes of this paper a less systematic approach will need to be adopted, given the massive problems of defining and measuring both market participation and financial performance accurately. Instead, the paper will concentrate on certain aspects of industry conduct and consider how far these match up to half a dozen attributes which one would expect, *a priori*, an increasingly competitive industry to manifest[6].

One would expect:

- firms in a competitive banking industry to identify and fill gaps in the range of services provided or of customers served;
- product prices (including interest rates) to bear a close and predictable relationship to costs (including capital costs);
- cartelised agreements and restrictive practices, whether or not officially sanctioned, to become untenable;
- firms to be less hidebound by traditional perceptions of institutional roles and thus more willing to diversify (or indeed specialise) in search of competitive advantage;
- to see more financial transactions undertaken directly between principals on efficient financial markets rather than via financial intermediaries; and
- traditionally bundled services to be unbundled.

Though the evidence is far from clear-cut, and differs both within and between national banking systems, there seems little doubt that competitive conduct in recent years has accorded to a considerable extent with what theory would lead one to expect.

(i) The opening up of banking systems to competitive forces has indeed resulted in a major process of spectrum-filling, as participants have identified and plugged gaps in, *inter alia*, the maturity of the deposit and credit instruments on offer, the range of currencies in which those instruments are available, the amounts in which they are available, and the types of customers to whom they are extended. Of particular significance has been the development of options and other so-called derivative instruments, since the more efficient markets that exist in such instruments the less banks may be called upon to play their traditional role of financial transformation: markets will take over the banks' function of transforming short-term, low-risk deposits into long-term, high-risk loans, for example.

(ii) As already noted, increased competition has made it hard for the established banks to maintain the high degree of cross-subsidisation that characterised their pricing behaviour in less competitive times. To give just one example, as long as the credit card segment of the market was the province of the major clearing banks, it was possible for them to operate a charging structure in which those customers who availed themselves of expensive extended credit facilities subsidised those who did not; the arrival of new card issuers eventually rendered that policy untenable.

(iii) Competitive forces have made it increasingly hard for traditional players to maintain industry-level agreements, even where these do not fall foul of restrictive practices legislation. For example, the major UK banks originally agreed to adopt an industry-level approach to the introduction of electronic funds transfer at the point of sale, and had indeed progressed a long way down this collaborative road before competitive pressures within their own ranks forced the abandonment of that policy.

(iv) The recent institutional history of the banking industry has been dominated by essays in diversification. This of course has been a consequence, not only of competitive forces, but also of deregulation, though it should not be forgotten that much of the recent financial deregulation has itself been a (sometimes belated) response to competitive pressures to which the regulators have had to yield. For instance, the deregulation that allowed banks to participate in the UK securities industry in 1986 was at least partly a consequence of the competition that the Stock Exchange was facing from the United States.

(It is only to be expected that participants in a competitive industry will seek to diversify within or even beyond the boundaries of that industry, particularly if they have previously been inhibited by custom or practice from doing so. The desire to meet a wide range of their customers' financial needs, and to harvest economies of scope in the process, is a natural and benign feature of competitive rivalry. It does not of course follow that all such essays are bound to succeed; indeed it is almost axiomatic that in a truly competitive market some at least of them will not. The tendency to overestimate the benefits and underestimate the risks of diversification seems to be a well-nigh universal one, by no means confined to the banking industry. With the industry as a whole now going through leaner times, the emphasis of competitive strategy can be expected to shift from diversification to specialisation, as firms seek to focus more closely on products and markets where they enjoy distinctive competences.)

(v)   Arguably, of most far-reaching concern to established banks, the expected shift from institutions to markets, has taken place on a significant scale. Dramatic evidence of the trend can be seen in the US corporate finance market, where the share of US companies' annual borrowing needs met by banks fell from nearly 50 per cent to barely three per cent between 1980 and 1987, as companies met their financing needs by issuing marketable securities instead. Some of this trend has of course already proved cyclical: there is always a tendency for business to move from banks to markets in good times and back to banks in hard times. But the combination of deregulation, technological change and greater competitive rivalry has almost certainly prompted an irreversible flow of financial intermediation from banks to markets.

(In passing, it is worth noting that this shift of business from banks to markets may well be operationally more efficient, by "cutting out the middleman", while at the same time being informationally less efficient: diffuse participants in securities markets lack the access to accurate information about a company's position and prospects that a relationship banker usually enjoys.)

(vi)   There has been some unbundling of hitherto composite banking services, caused at least in part by the opening up of niches in the banking market to outside competition and the consequential undermining of cross-subsidisation. We have already noted how a consumer loan can be unbundled, or deconstructed, into its component parts. Other examples of unbundling include the introduction of separate charges for ancillary services such as managerial advice or safe custody, and the provision of corporate account information as a distinctive service from money transmission. The nature of banking, however, limits the extent to which unbundling can be expected to proceed: for instance, while the transmission of funds between accounts may be conceptually separate from the creation of credits and debits on those accounts, they are for all practical purposes part of the same (current account) service. There is also evidence that some customers prefer the convenience and predictability of bundled services, while the inter-temporal nature of many banking services undoubtedly helps to sustain both bundling and cross-subsidisation.

9. The Costs of Competition

The evidence of how far intensified competition in banking has been reflected in changes in structure, conduct and performance, of the kind that economic theory would lead one to expect, is inevitably tentative and impressionistic at this stage, if only because the new competitive dynamics are still working their way through the system. Robust conclusions about the consequences of competition must therefore be deferred. There is, however, one general observation which should be made before concluding.

In an uncertain world it is inevitable that the unleashing of competitive forces onto a hither uncompetitive market will produce turbulence: the more potent those forces, and the more ossified the status quo, the greater that turbulence is likely to be. The reasons are obvious enough. Managers must rapidly reformulate their objectives, taking into account the likely behaviour of their customers and their existing and potential competitors in the process. It is small wonder if the market assumptions on which those objectives are based are not always borne out, or if the firms prove incapable of meeting the standards of performance which those objectives entail.

A particular feature of such turbulence is likely to be a tendency for firms to "overshoot" as they attempt to adjust their asset portfolios in response to new competitive opportunities. That is to say, the sum of their individual portfolio objectives will tend to exceed the quantity of available business (mortgage lending or securities trading, to take two topical examples) that the market as a whole is capable of sustaining.

This tendency is not unconnected with the widely observed "herd instinct", by which participants in an increasingly competitive market, pursuing similar objectives and armed with near-identical market information, unsurprisingly tend to take the same decisions at the same time. The likelihood of such behaviour will be all the greater if, as is often the case in the financial services industry, the managerial penalties for being out of line and wrong outweigh the managerial rewards for being out of line and right.

So, as indicated much earlier in this paper, there is no reason to assume that the consequences of enhanced competition in banking will all be benign; in the short to medium term deleterious consequences for banks, customers and the public good may be quite considerable. For instance, there is little doubt that the competitive response to financial deregulation in the 1980s involved an excessively rapid expansion of consumer credit, which in its turn contributed to the overheating of the UK economy and the severity of the ensuing recession. Indeed, even in the longer term, problems of information asymmetry between firms and their investors could prove seriously destabilising, if the role of banks as information-holding intermediaries declines, although increased competitive pressures may help to stimulate higher standards of corporate disclosure[7].

In such circumstances the temptation to reimpose constraints on competitive behaviour, such as credit controls, is understandable. As already stated, in a world of market imperfections it cannot be assumed that increasing competitiveness in one particular market will necessarily increase economic welfare. At the very least there may be a temptation to adopt gradualist rather than "big bang" approaches to deregulation. This seems to be the preferred approach of the UK Building Societies Commission. In other parts of the system, however, it must be questioned whether regulators actually have the power to manage gradual changes in market conditions any more. Once on the tiger of increased competition and deregulation, it is very hard to dismount.

In any case, the more important lesson to be drawn from the experience of competitive turbulence is surely that it is extremely dangerous to allow competitive forces to be dammed up for too long. A more competitive banking market may not bring in its train all the benefits an economics textbook might lead one to expect; but, given a reasonable time to settle down, it is likely to prove a good deal preferable to the alternative.

1. This concept was first explored in any detail by J M Clark in a seminal paper, 'Towards a concept of workable competition', reprinted in *Readings in the Social Control of Industry*, American Economics Association, 1942. See also S H Sosnick, 'A Critique of Concepts of Workable Competition', *Quarterly Journal of Economics*, Vol 52, 1958.
2. The seminal work is W J Baumol, 'Contestable Markets: An Uprising in the Theory of Industry Structure', *American Economic Review*, vol 72, 1982.
3. Nevertheless, even in Japan there has been a marked shift in recent years from (domestic) bank to (overseas) market-based finance. For a review of recent trends see L E Crabbe et al, 'Recent Developments in Corporate Finance', *Federal Reserve Bulletin*, August 1990.
4. For a review of the empirical evidence, see M K Lewis and M T Davis, 'Domestic and International Banking', Chapter 7, Philip Allan, 1987.
5. The competitive implications of the Basle arrangements are considered in D T Llewellyn, 'Basle Capital Convergence Arrangements: The Strategic Dilemma of World Banking', *Repères*, Banque Internationale à Luxembourg, No 23, 1990.
6. For propounding these *a priori* expectations, I am indebted to my colleague Professor David Llewellyn.
7. From the substantial literature on information and finance, particularly relevant contributions are O E Williamson, 'Costly Monitoring, Financial Intermediation and Equilibrium Credit Rationing', *Journal of Monetary Economics*, 1986, and H E Leland & D H Pyle, 'Informational Asymmetries, Financial Structure and Financial Intermediation', *Journal of Finance*, May 1977.

Organizational Changes in Banking — A Case Study

Hilmar Kopper
*Spokesman of the
Board of Managing
Directors
Deutsche Bank*

Hilmar Kopper

Hilmar Kopper was born in 1935 in Oslanin. After high-school, he completed an apprenticeship with Deutsche Bank in Cologne. He was a management trainee with J. Henry Schroder Banking Corporation, New York, before joining the Foreign Department of Deutsche Bank's Central Office in Dusseldorf. In 1960, he moved to Leverkusen branch where he became manager in 1969. From 1972 to 1974, he served as a member of the Board of Managing Directors of European Asian Bank.

In 1975, Mr. Kopper was appointed executive vice-president of Deutsche Bank AG, and became a member of the Board of Managing Directors in 1977. In December 1989, he was elected spokesman of the Board of Managing Directors of Deutsche Bank AG.

Hilmar Kopper serves as chairman of the Supervisory Board of Daimler-Benz AG and Klockner-Humboldt-Deutz AG, and as member of the Supervisory Board of a number of companies such as Akzo NV, Bayer AG, Deutsche Lufthansa AG, Mannesmann AG, Munich Re AG, Solvay SA and Veba AG as well as non-executive director of Pilkington plc.

Contents

Erratum

Page 63, section 1, 1st paragraph, line 11 should read
"ratio of inhabitants per banking outlet".

62

Introduction

During the last few months a number of international banks have reshaped their organizational structure. This has been due largely to changes in the marketplace. The banking industry has come under scrutiny as regards control mechanisms and organizational aptitude to cope with risk, be it externally in the marketplace or internally within the organization. Even the three big Swiss banks, together with Deutsche Bank the only remaining Triple-A rated banks, have begun to take a long look at themselves. Credit Suisse decided to build a holding structure. UBS recently announced a reorganization which split its board and management into two parts: one responsible for specific product groups and the other responsible for various regions. Finally, Swiss Bank Corporation announced during the course of last year that it is reorganizing mainly its international activities. To a famous German economist of the turn of the century, Schmalenbach, this would not come as a surprise, as he stated back in 1910 that "all that is considered to be the organizational structure of a bank is in fact a command system and bureaucracy that developed by accident without a pronounced trace of general characteristics and an underlying concept. I (that is, Schmalenbach) always had the impression that this development reflected the possibility that the whole organization might eventually go bankrupt".

1. The Changing Marketplace for Banks

The regulated environment of the 1930s set the scene for banking operations well into the 1950s. The late 1960s witnessed deregulation (in Germany through the 1967 reforms of Karl Schiller principally as regards interest on bank balances), which led to intensive price-competition, something completely new to the industry. In the 1970s new target markets were discovered, such as retail customers. But competition remained largely oligopolistic. In 1957, Germany had 13,000 bank branches, by 1967 the number had doubled and in 1990 there were over 48,300 (44,000 without the former East Germany). Germany has the highest density of banking outlets, measured by the ratio of customers per banking outlet (1,400, compared to 2,600 in the UK, 2,700 in Japan and 4,300 in the USA). By now one can say that the German market is overbanked.

The 1980s witnessed a rapid expansion abroad as free competition and globalization opened up established market structures. It was no longer possible to speak of a fairly homogeneous supply of banking products, as new entrants, including non-banks, and the increasing sophistication of large and multinational corporations in particular, changed the traditional intermediation function of banks. In the past decade, which may be called the era of investment banking, a range of revolutionary products caused bankers to change from "bank officials" to financial engineers. The historical perspective underlines the changes from a seller's market to a buyer's market and from oligopolistic to entirely free competition.

Corporate institutions, be they companies or banks, continuously evolve in the economic process. Banks have some micro-economic particularities. "Production" and distribution have to be seen as an entity, as a bank's services are only generated upon completion. Only the mandate for and then execution of a transaction creates value. Service industries do not "store" products in inventory. "Production" is a function of bank staff so that economies of scale are based on individual efficiency. The latter will show itself only upon execution of a banking transaction. Hence, any service organization faces a problem of establishing and allocating costs to the generation and execution of products as well as performing a bottom line calculation for individual customers. According to McKinsey studies, probably only less than a quarter of total costs can be allocated directly, 20-30% being pure overhead, the remainder being unaccounted for.

Another development that made organizations increasingly complex is the cross-fertilization and creation of synergies — in principle to be encouraged — that makes accountability even more difficult. Different business areas may as a consequence cross-subsidize each other, ie losses in one being compensated by the other and vice versa. For example, advantageous re-financing due to cheap deposits may make loans on the asset-side more price-competitive; fee and interest income may overcompensate losses in other business areas such as non-documentary payments; losses made in doing business with one customer are compensated by profits made with another. These cross-subsidies work as long as market demand has no choice. When customers do have a choice, they can go elsewhere and remove one side of the equation. For example, commercial paper sold to investors substituted to a large extent short-term bank financing and money market funds eroded the cheap refinancing base of savings and loans associations in the US.

Hence the need to change. To quote Rosabeth Moss Kanter:

"change masters" are "those people and organizations adept at the art of anticipating the need for, and learning, productive change".† "Copy-cat strategies" that simply follow others, as in the days of oligopolistic markets, are not enough.

In order to initiate change, it is paramount to single out strengths and weaknesses. Customer segments and products have to be analysed according to criteria of profitability and growth potential. This does not take place in a vacuum as one has to take account of the triangular relationship of bank-customer-competitor. When competing with specialist institutions such as investment banks, universal banks will have to be innovative in order to unbundle and rebundle products in different ways to deliver "portfolio-combinations" on the basis of a competitive ratio of price and output. It is the value-added for the customer that counts. Strategies of cost-leadership or high value-added have to be based, however, on a clear definition of customer segments. Private banking is more easily defined in terms of retail banking and services for high net worth individuals. Corporate finance, however, is more likely to be organized along product lines, whilst a regional organization is more likely for overseas and branch operations. Complex organizations are, therefore, likely to have multi-point matrix systems.

It is this complexity that keeps bankers busy these days. Many banks had to review their activities in order to find the optimal product mix and delivery system, this being no static process but a dynamic one. They all were or still are facing the same basic problems of organizational structures and potential friction within: the difficulty of co-ordinating various market activities combined with communication and integration problems stemming especially from international activities:

- The globalization of financial markets has been a tremendous stimulant in that global competition in the 1980s has forced the banking industry to align itself. This was induced further by deregulation, soaring costs and narrowing margins.
- The role of technology has lowered transformation costs and increased efficiency, whilst at the same time blurring product lines. However, increased volatility also means greater opportunities.
- Universal banks are multi-product, multi-client institutions that operate in many areas which differ widely in terms of product, market and key success factors. Hence, a customized approach is

† *The Change Masters: Corporate Entrepreneurs at Work*, Allen & Unwin, 1984

necessary. New products or organizational units alone are not able to give a bank a sustainable competitive advantage. Today universal banks are competing with a growing number of small, highly specialized, innovative and very flexible players.

■ One of the major assets of a bank is the quality of its people on whose performance it ultimately depends. Its staff needs to be organized in such a way that it can freely develop and use individual capabilities and skills. A challenging environment does not preclude team-work. However, a system of reward by merit needs to make the system accountable in a more or less objective fashion.

2. What is Organizational Change?

In its purest form it could mean the adaptation of an organizational structure by innovating the products one offers and the process by which one delivers. This is achieved, not only by setting up "physical" structures, but by modelling relationships, hierarchies and work patterns, ie people. This is all the more important for banks as human-capital-intensive producers. People constitute the most important input and asset. Hence organizations have to relearn constantly ie to encourage people to use possibly neglected creative capabilities in order to tap the potent economic stimulus of "idea power".

The environment will condition the opportunities to do so. Problems have to be approached in an integrative fashion, so important for universal banks, in embracing ideas from possibly even unconnected sources in order to streamline internal processes or deliver products to cater to the needs of diverse groups of customers. This contrasts with a segmentalist style which is anti-change-oriented as it compartmentalizes issues too much. Specialist biases, hierarchy and political conflicts are more likely to inhibit innovation and organizational adaptation in a segmentalist institution. George Bernard Shaw may go a little far in saying in *The Devil's Disciple* that "the worst sin towards our fellow creatures is not to hate them, but to be indifferent to them; that's the essence of inhumanity", but the message is clear.

3. Different Approaches

An ongoing, integrative response has shown significant differences in approach between various organizational models, although there are some similarities.

66

In general these are:

■ Whilst recognizing the all-important home market that provides a base to venture abroad, a stronger emphasis is placed on activities outside the home market in the context of globalization of financial services.

■ Clearer distribution of management responsibility in order to improve entrepreneurship within, often called intrapreneurship, as an answer to the deterioration of margins, shorter product cycles, the need for enhanced innovation and the resulting, growing complexity of bank management.

■ The search for flat hierarchical structures combined with the delegation of more responsibility and decision-making in line functions in order to be close to the customer. This in turn will enable anticipatory product design, shorter lead time and increasingly targeted marketing. It will change behaviour from a re-active to pro-active mode.

■ Freeing top-management from day-to-day operational responsibilities in order for it to focus on strategic issues. Many large companies and banks are in danger of being over-managed and under-led. The board, and particularly the chief executive, must introduce a clear sense of direction and prioritize issues when formulating strategy.

4. The Deutsche Bank Experience

Deutsche Bank decided to restructure its organization about two years ago. So far only the domestic operations have been restructured. Deutsche Bank's foreign operations have already followed more up-to-date structures in its local environments. They will be reviewed after successful implementation of the new domestic structure.

The steps followed and the underlying reasoning can be summarized as follows:

■ Distinct customer-oriented strategies and approaches are to provide for . . .

■ more decision-making and know-how close to the customer, supported by . . .

■ continuous dialogue of the customer side with products generators, thus creating . . .

■ organizational synergies through the pursuit of an integrative change process, which will result in . . .

- enhanced internal communication and avoidance of segmentalist behaviour, which will . . .
- increase marketing and sales effectiveness as well as innovation, which in turn is the precondition for . . .
- improved profitability of all its business activities in all regions.

Today customers want "standard products" at the lowest possible cost, but also expect comprehensive and expert service and advice on complicated transactions. Banks must be prepared on both counts. They must deliver low-cost, standardized products for the general banking customers and tailored products for the more demanding corporate and private clients. Complex products like swaps, caps, financial futures, cross-border leasing or forward rate agreements are becoming more and more common and now have a firm place in the range of services of every major international bank.

Deutsche Bank responded to this trend towards specialization by acquiring or setting up subsidiaries, such as Morgan Grenfell, a small private domestic bank, to cater for very demanding high-net worth individuals, a building society and a life insurance business, as well as by forming special project groups such as the so-called Liquidity Group (for short-term liquidity management for institutions and corporates) and DB Export Leasing. But that is not enough. Following an analysis of our position in Germany and in the world, combined with an investigation of future demands put on the bank, the Board decided to review and reshape the overall organization. It wanted to give the bank as a whole a forward-looking orientation which would allow for the drawing on specialized "centres of competence" whilst preserving the advantages of "universal banking".

The thinking centred largely on the question of how one should shape the relationship between a regional and a divisional structure. Until this point, regional areas of responsibility had predominated in the Deutsche Bank organization. Although this structure was a good solution for creating synergies all over the bank, it was found suboptimal in terms of clear customer and profit responsibility. Marketing strategies were difficult to implement throughout the bank. The growing importance of specialized head office departments and subsidiaries as "centres of competence" meant that regional responsibility was not enough. At a time when Germany will only be one among several regions in our future European home market, a time characterized by the growing internationalization and rising mobility of our customers, stronger emphasis must be placed on customer orientation at all levels in the bank.

Any new structure had to conform to the values and the "mission" of Deutsche Bank:

■ firstly, Deutsche Bank is relationship-oriented. That means, a new organization will have to enable the meeting of specific clients needs and provide for distinct customer-oriented strategies and approaches;

■ secondly, the belief in the concept of universality. This universality must be supported through a homogeneous strategy, the management of synergies between resources, a strong corporate identity and, wherever possible, the using of cross-selling effects;

■ thirdly, it was decided to keep the system of decentralized management by objectives;

■ fourthly, it was felt that the regional basis is and will remain a strong success factor.

5. Arriving at a New Organizational Model

A working group was put in charge of the initial brain-storming, consisting of in-house line- and staff-people and assisted by outside consultants. They discussed the principles of a possible new organization for months. The framework had been established by the definition of the following objectives:

■ Creation of management structures and reporting systems that allow for company-wide implementation of business policies.

■ Specialization in terms of products and services to meet the challenge of sophisticated competitors.

■ Establishment of clearly defined responsibilities for profits (sales and costs) at all management levels to promote entrepreneurial thinking.

■ Support of authority which matches responsibility and makes managers accountable.

■ Transparency of individual performance through modern reporting systems to measure results, detect strengths and weaknesses and to initiate adequate steps where units or managers perform below standard or expectations.

This looks somewhat like the "five commandments". It is, of course, less dramatic than it sounds. The new structure was not supposed to undermine the bank's ongoing traditional values or its identity as a universal bank. From the very beginning, therefore, the intention was not to carry out a structural or "cultural" revolution, but rather to adjust established structures to new requirements on the basis of traditional strengths.

What finally emerged were two alternatives: complete divisionalization or "corporate business and service units". Chart No 1 summarizes the main characteristics of both concepts.

(See Chart No 1 on page 75)

A complete divisionalization would mean:
■ creating divisions, like "banks in the bank" which are able to operate widely on a stand-alone basis, the next logical step being a holding organization;
■ fitting nearly all resources into these divisions; and
■ the optimization of synergies would be a divisional task.

The concept of forming corporate groups would have the following implications:
■ These corporate groups would be profit centres, but would be tied together by corporate functions such as planning and control, shared resources etc.
■ Administration, EDP, personnel and controlling could be managed as shared resources.
■ Therefore synergies could be optimized throughout the corporate groups.

The next step was to rate these alternatives according the their functionality and their ability to meet corporate goals. Chart No 2 summarizes the result.

(See Chart No 2 on page 76)

■ Compared with the old organization both concepts allow for a better alignment of the bank to the key success factors of the business units.
■ Both concepts support a stronger "self-interest" of the business units. Subsidies and compensation of losses in one unit by profits in another are now quite apparent (if at all taking place).
■ Cost transparency was supported by both concepts, but complete divisionalization would mean giving up fruitful synergies.
■ The most important difference between the concepts is their answer to the question of which one is best in supporting, not only better strategic and operational manoeuvrability of the bank, but

also the question of preserving proven structures and values. With the concept of complete divisionalization the potential danger for the bank's unity loomed large and had to be avoided. The concept of forming business groups, however, maintains both clear profit responsibility and the unity of the bank through shared resources, service agreements, job rotation and a better view of the whole.

6. Implementing Organizational Change

To put it in a nutshell, the matrix was turned by 90 degrees. From being a more regionally-oriented structure with broad horizontal scope more emphasis was put on vertical divisions without adopting a purely "scientific" divisionalized scheme. The potential drawbacks of a holding structure were avoided as this is more likely to lead to lost synergies and in-house competition.

The new organizational structure is reflected in the responsibilities of the board of managing directors of Deutsche Bank. Corporate business and service groups were created which basically already existed before: private customers, corporate customers and institutions, and support services. In future, therefore, there will be a Private Banking Group, a Corporate/Institutional Banking Group and a Resources and Controlling Group.

(See Chart No 3 on page 77)

Within these corporate groups, business divisions and service divisions will be set up. Since the overall co-ordination of activities and strategic policymaking in the corporate groups will be handled by the members of the Board of Managing Directors responsible for the respective corporate group, they will also have profit and loss responsibility for their respective customer and/or product group, and the quality and cost efficiency of the services they provide. Board members continue to have regional responsibilities, however. Hence one deviated from the principle of divisional responsibility in the Institutional and Corporate Banking/Finance Divisions in as much as the member of the Board of Managing Directors responsible for the region will continue to have primary customer responsibility. It is believed that relationship management and personal contacts — not least through members of the Board as ultimate account managers — are decisive for good results in this business. The Private Banking Group was divided up into two divisions focused on customer groups.

71

The Retail Banking Division is responsible for business with the large number of private retail customers and small corporate customers, while the Private Banking Division caters for the needs of high net-worth individuals with more sophisticated products and more individualized service. The Corporate/Institutional Banking Group comprises the Corporate Banking Division and Financial Institutions Division, both of which are defined by customer groups, and the product-related divisions Corporate Finance, Securities Trading and Sales, Asset Management, Foreign Exchange, Money Market and Precious Metals Trading, and Morgan Grenfell. The latter is not part of the corporate finance group, but is run as an independent and autonomous "centre of competence". Thus, the matrix represents a hybrid as divisions justify their existence on the basis of both customer and product responsibility.

The Resources and Controlling Group consists of the five service divisions: Treasury, Credit Control, Personnel, Administration and Operations, and finally Controlling. They have service and cost responsibility within the framework of their support functions for the business divisions. The service division "Controlling" will provide the management information in a newly-developed management information system based on the corporate groups and business divisions.

As business divisions need support at the highest level, responsibility for individual business areas was maintained and enforced at the board level. This does not mean involvement of the board member in daily duties. A director is there to ensure that sound strategy has been formulated, and that this strategy is consistent with corporate guidelines for that division as to domain, risk levels, target results and the like. In addition, he or she will select capable executives or, if necessary, remove them. He has to insist that tough actions are taken if necessary, but also reward for outstanding performance. It is also his or her task to ensure adequate control systems. He will give final approval on very large transactions that may affect the future of the division. Finally he will serve as a sounding board, asking discerning questions and providing objective advice.

In most cases, the new divisions are entities which already exist today at Head Office and in the branch network, but in future will be "rebundled" and managed differently. In the future structure, therefore, certain names will no longer be found and new ones will appear. The Real Estate Finance and Development Department was split up between the Private Banking, Corporate Banking and

Corporate Finance Divisions. The previous Asset Management Groups will be integrated into the Private Banking Division. The Central International Department forms the core of the new Financial Institutions Division. The former investment banking activities were reinforced by experts from the former Central International Department, and for some months now has been working as the Corporate Finance Division. Also new is the Morgan Grenfell/M&A Division, which is responsible for our M&A business worldwide.

This new structure was introduced to staff early this year. Senior executives had been heavily involved in meetings and were always up-to-date in the process in an effort to avoid the trappings of a seg-mentalist organization, where no one has real information on upper management thinking. The aim was to shake things up whilst at the same time maintaining a measure of security and understanding. One is well aware that individuals do not do "big things" but that team-work still counts. After all, individual actions are less important than the cumulative accomplishments that eventually result in "big" performance for the bank.

The regional organization at a branch level roughly corresponds to the structure of the Board of Managing Directors.

(See Chart No 4 on page 78)

Depending on the size of the operation, each principal branch office will have approximately three-five or maybe even six regional managers. As a general rule, there will be at least one regional manager "Retail Banking", one regional manager responsible for corporate business and another for support functions ("Resources and Controlling"). They will have at least one deputy.

Similar to the Board's overall responsibility, each regional manager has to assume "primary" or profit responsibility for the operation of the division in his region. The regional management group will decide jointly on all issues where the region as a whole is concerned — especially on issues dealing with the allocation of regional resources, public representation and so on. Individual per-formance assessments of regional managers will be based primarily on the results of their divisions, without neglecting the performance of the region as a whole.

7. Summary

The new division-oriented structure aims at strengthening the profit and cost responsibility of management. Activities within the Deutsche Bank Group are to become more transparent, measurable and therefore easier to manage. The board wants to promote entrepreneurship at all levels and encourage and reward creativity and initiative. It is believed that future success will depend on greater commitment to target groups and corresponding products, more focused marketing and cost efficiency. The aim of the changes, therefore, is to align the bank's structure more closely with the market and enhance its profit orientation.

The new structure has already been successfully implemented, on a trial basis, in the Frankfurt, Freiburg and Cologne branch regions. Based on this experience, the overall concept was adjusted and refined. Implementation of the new structure in all domestic regions commenced at the beginning of this year. In the foreword to the organizational compendium, the Board of Managing Directors has summarized its thinking as follows: "The new organization represents an important step in the development of our bank. Even though much was already under way — thanks to markets and competitors — many things are still new and unfamiliar. Familiar names, established reporting channels, traditional structures will be changed. A structural reform is uncomfortable — and has to be. How else could one get things moving? And we have to keep moving so that the bank can maintain its competitive position in the long run. This does not mean permanent reform or revolutionary upheaval, but keeping pace, carefully, with evolutionary development. If, with this in mind, we accept the reform as a positive challenge and use the opportunities it offers, we shall be successful. We need more transparency, more responsibility and more market orientation, and we want to bring together accountability, function and responsibility at a level close to the market. We want — and call upon — our staff to think and act like entrepreneurs."

Two alternative solutions: Complete divisionalization vs. creating corporate groups
– Main characteristics of both concepts –

Complete Divisionalization	Creating Corporate Groups
• Far-reaching, stand alone operating divisions (Banks in the bank)	• Corporate groups with profit responsibility are tied together by corporate planning, shared resources etc.
• Basically all resources are folded into divisions	• Organisation, EDP, Personal and Controlling will be managed as shared resources
• Optimalization of synergies in the divisions	• Synergies should be optimized throughout the corporate groups

Chart No 1

Forming Corporate Groups is the better organizational concept
— Comparison of Alternatives —

Goal to aim for		Status quo	Complete Divisionalization	Forming of Corporate Groups
1	Commitment to Target Groups Alignment to success factors of the market	⊖	⊕	⊕
2	Cutting down cross-subsidies between products and clients	⊖	⊕	⊕
3	Better cost-transparency and more effective cost-management	⊖	⊕ / ⊖	⊕
4	Preparing better manoeuvrability of the bank	⊖	⊖	⊕
	Maintaining the bank's unity	⊕	⊖	⊕

Chart No 2

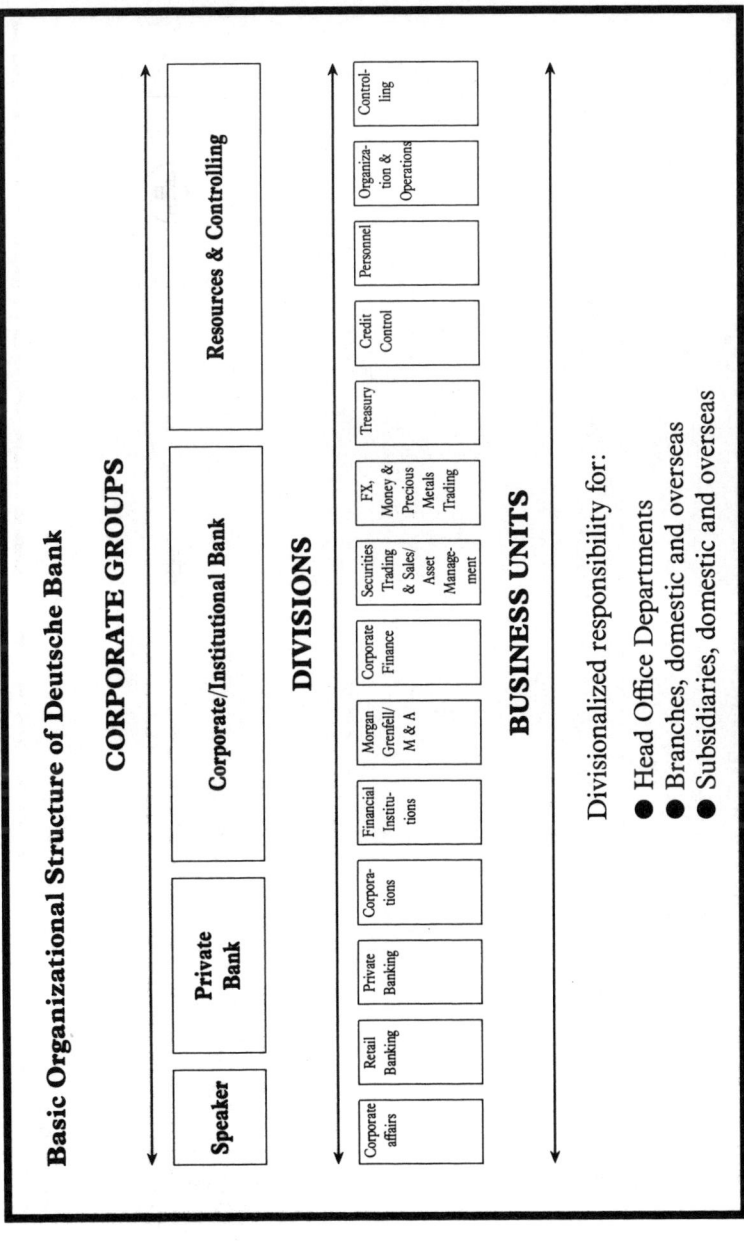

Basic Organizational Structure of Deutsche Bank

CORPORATE GROUPS

| Speaker | Private Bank | Corporate/Institutional Bank | Resources & Controlling |

DIVISIONS

| Corporate affairs | Retail Banking | Private Banking | Corpora- tions | Financial Institu- tions | Morgan Grenfell/ M & A | Corporate Finance | Securities Trading & Sales/ Asset Manage- ment | FX, Money & Precious Metals Trading | Treasury | Credit Control | Personnel | Organiza- tion & Operations | Control- ling |

BUSINESS UNITS

Divisionalized responsibility for:

● Head Office Departments
● Branches, domestic and overseas
● Subsidiaries, domestic and overseas

Chart No 3

Organizational Structure of a Regional Head Branch

Management of Regional Head Branch	Retail Banking	Private Banking	Corporations		Resources & Controlling
	Regional Manager (SVP)	Regional Manager (SVP)	Regional Mgr (SVP) 1 Medium-sized Corporations	Regional Mgr (SVP) 2 MNCs	Regional Manager (SVP)
	Marketing & Sales Management	Marketing & Sales Management	Marketing & Sales Management	Marketing & Sales Management	Legal
		Securities Trading & Sales	Credit Control	Foreign	Personnel
					Organization & Operations
					Controlling

Chart No 4

The Technology Response

Ronald Price
*Managing Director,
Group Operations,
Midland Bank*

Ronald Price

Ronald Price was born in 1938 and qualified as an electrical engineer, moving into computers while he was with the General Electric Company. He joined Urwick Orr and Partners in 1966, specialising in information technology as a management consultant, and becoming a partner in 1973.

In 1974, he moved to Hill Samuel, where he was responsible for information technology in the investment banking field. In 1975, he joined British Airways as head of consultancy.

He joined Midland Bank in 1985, initially as head of Group Systems and then as Group Computer Operations director. He became director of Group Information Technology in May 1989. He is a member of the Group Executive Committee.

Ronald Price is responsible for all operations activities throughout the Group, including banking operations, information technology, card services and property.

Contents

Appendices

Introduction

"Information Technology (IT) has had more impact on more fundamentals, more quickly, than virtually any other external change in the history of the banking industry. It is transforming every aspect of a bank's business, from its management information to the nature of the products and services it offers. It fundamentally affects many of the key drivers of both cost and revenue which will increasingly determine a bank's overall profitability and competitive position."

IMF Conference, 1989

This statement shows that IT is the key to the way we manage our banking business. Without good IT we do not have a good banking business. Yet banking is currently going through fundamental changes all over the world, especially in the UK, Europe and the USA. Therefore, if we are going to be successful, we had better be sure we are well placed to get the best from our IT professionals to meet, and take advantage of, these changes. To ensure that we get a satisfactory "technology response" we must be sure that:

- IT works in *support* of the business
- IT is well managed

Today, these are fundamental business requirements of any successful bank. This paper suggests ways in which these requirements can be met. First, though, some "scene-setting".

1. Overview of IT Phases in Banking

1.1 Phase 1 — Automation of Bank Office, 1960-1979

This phase enabled major banks to handle large and increasing volumes of activity without correspondingly proportionate increases in manpower. IT tackled the routine transaction processing, whilst the marketplace matured with more and more people using bank accounts. In the UK automation was used to handle:

- 27 million current accounts
- 17 million deposit accounts
- 12,000 branches
- over 3 billion cheques per annum

IT replaced conventional accounting machines and was typically linking the branch network into a large central computer.

1.2 Phase 2 — A Time of Transition, 1980 to date

This was the period in which the IT industry started to mature in the way it served banking:

- With the rapid development of data communications it became possible to run systems on-line and "realtime", thus opening up opportunities for some customers, especially corporates, to have direct access to a bank's products.
- "More bang per buck" by the hardware manufacturers saw the unit cost of computers begin to fall sharply, with personal computers harnessing the processing power seen only in mainframe computers in the 1960s. This made it possible to develop IT-based banking products in a wider variety than seen previously.
- Database management techniques became highly developed, making it possible to develop systems in a much more integrated way, using source data, entered only once, for a variety of different banking services.
- Users of IT became more IT aware and more literate on how IT could be used to add value to their businesses. We see many examples in banking today of IT users playing a much larger part in the development of new IT-based systems; some even write their own programs.

All these relatively recent developments have combined to produce a foundation for the banking industry to gather itself to use IT in aggressive ways to develop systems for new banking products which are bringing in revenues and gaining strategic competitive advantage. IT-literate bankers using personal computers linked to large central computers holding large corporate data bases have proved to be a very powerful combination.

1.3 Phase 3 — The Future

With increasing competition from *within* the industry we are (especially in the UK) facing an increasing degree of overcapacity. The banks which will survive will be those which use IT to go for economies of scale and become lowest cost producers. At the same time, IT will increasingly pose a threat to the banking industry. It can be used to reduce barriers for entry into the marketplace by those organisations which hitherto had not been regarded as in any way likely to encroach on traditional banking territories. IT enables market segmentation and "cherry picking" by non-banking organisations which possess their own powerful and professional IT organisations.

New markets will emerge through the use of IT. The globalisation of financial markets would not be possible without IT. New emerging technologies such as Image Processing and EDI (Electronic Data Interchange) are currently being developed and will prove to be extremely important to the banking industry. We ignore them at our peril, because outside competitors certainly are and will be exploiting them and attacking our more traditional markets; also they will offer great opportunities to improve our products and services even further, giving greater customer value and, we hope, enabling banks to reduce costs even further. More about these two developments later.

The challenge for the banks will be to spot which organisations are likely to pose the threats and head them off by developing their own new capabilities at the right price. Threats can come from such organisations as:
- building societies
- IT vendors themselves
- retailers
- major corporations.

Now, more than ever, banks really do have to answer the question, "what business are we really in?".

The challenge for the "traditional" bankers will be to:
- develop their sales capabilities to develop an increasingly sophisticated customer base;
- develop their own IT awareness so they can "spot" the market niches which IT can use to exploit and also so they can play a full part in developing the products/services to fit these markets.

The challenge for the IT professionals will be to:
- develop their banking business awareness so they can work fully in partnership with the business;
- improve their speed of response. It still takes too long to deliver a fully-worked system to a set of eager business users; and
- get the system right, first time! Banking history has too many examples of abandoned IT projects, often large, which have proven expensive and, more importantly, have lost valuable time in the competitive world that all banks face.

Having "set the scene", the remainder of this paper describes how bankers and IT professionals can ensure that IT is responsive to meeting the business challenge.

2. Information Technology in Partnership with the Business

2.1 The IT Plan

Although IT has been around a long time, there are still many organisations today (not just in banking), in which the business professionals and IT professionals are working to different agendas. The business plans (if they exist) take no account of how IT can be exploited to add shareholder value; the IT plans (if *they* exist) are often too technical and incapable of being understood, and therefore cannot be endorsed by the bankers as affordable and meeting their business needs. The fault lies with both parties. What is needed is for IT to work in partnership with the business, with joint development of clear business plans, followed by joint development of IT plans, which align with the business.

In Midland, we believe that planning for technology in alignment with the business should address four factors:

Factor 1 — Business Mission for Value Creation
"Where should we invest?"

Factor 2 — Role of Technology in Supporting Achievement of Business Goals
"What should we expect technology to accomplish?"

Factor 3 — Health of Current Systems
"Do we need to re-invest?"

Factor 4 — Management Structure
"How do we manage technology delivery and the resulting change?"

This then helps us build the "tabs" of the IT plan, which are:

Chapter 1 — Vision for technology for the business

Chapter 2 — Technology objectives for support of competitive advantage for each business

Chapter 3 — Technology foundation/architecture for the business

Chapter 4 — Technology development plan for the business:
- projects
- priorities
- budgets
- timescale
- checkpoints

Chapter 5 — Plan for managing IT as an entity/division.

Figure 1 *(see page 87)* depicts how a jointly-developed business/IT plan should focus on value creation.

86

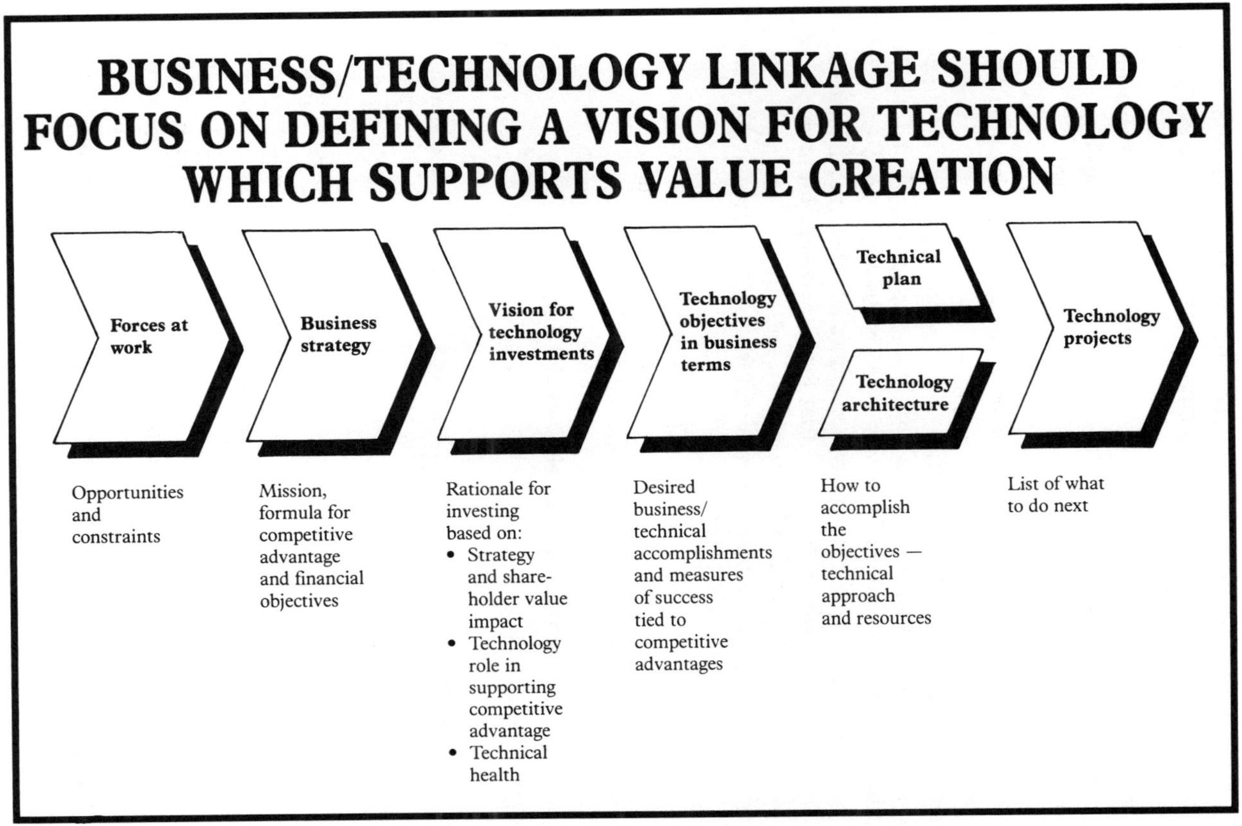

BUSINESS/TECHNOLOGY LINKAGE SHOULD FOCUS ON DEFINING A VISION FOR TECHNOLOGY WHICH SUPPORTS VALUE CREATION

Forces at work — Opportunities and constraints

Business strategy — Mission, formula for competitive advantage and financial objectives

Vision for technology investments — Rationale for investing based on:
- Strategy and shareholder value impact
- Technology role in supporting competitive advantage
- Technical health

Technology objectives in business terms — Desired business/technical accomplishments and measures of success tied to competitive advantages

Technical plan

Technology architecture — How to accomplish the objectives — technical approach and resources

Technology projects — List of what to do next

Figure 1

The resultant plan is developed iteratively (most important) between the business and IT and aims to give a clear direction to IT which:

- demonstrably supports and enables current and future business activities;
- is affordable;
- gives clear priorities;
- is achievable (ie not over ambitious in scope, cost or timescale);
- avoids duplication; and
- is simple and understandable.

To get to this point, much joint analytical work will be needed about the current state of IT health for each business area. Figures 2-5 *(see pages 89-92)* are illustrative examples of how in Midland we document the analyses to ensure that for each business unit we focus on the views of the business management regarding:

- the current state and potential for automation across the main areas of the business unit;
- their views on the current systems, with special regard to the functions and value for money they deliver; and
- the architectural issues surrounding the systems.

2.2 Getting Business Ownership of the Plan

It is important that the management of each strategic business unit "signs off" the part of the overall IT plan which serves them. It is then a question of deciding on a total Group basis if the plan is acceptable.

In Midland, we achieve this by ensuring that each strategic business unit (SBU) has contributed to the plan through its own representative, who is both knowledgeable about its business and IT literate; however, he is a businessman first and always. We call this person a Business Systems Manager. He is part of the SBU management team, reporting to the business rather than IT management.

To give approval/take decisions on the overall Group plan we have a Group IT Board. This is business-driven, and comprises eight senior executives of whom only two are senior IT people — the others are directors of major business areas within the bank. The role of this board, which approves projects greater than £2.5m, is to ensure that IT is adding shareholder value by virtue of:

- being applied to the right areas of the business;
- being managed professionally.

MM CORPORATE – CURRENT STATE OF AUTOMATION

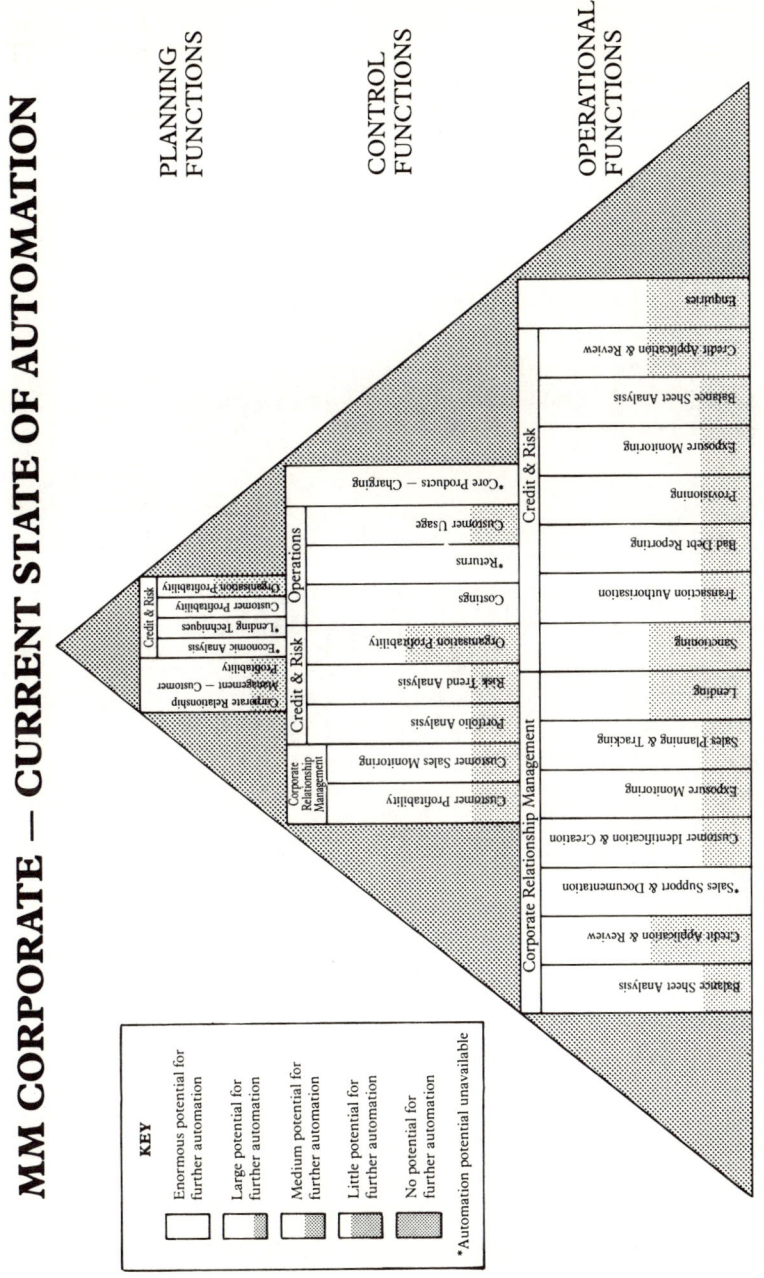

Figure 2

MIDLAND MONTAGU CORPORATE

SYSTEM	PLATFORM	LOSS IMPACT (1 WEEK)	IT COST PROD'N CHARGES	IT COST DEV/MAINT
GROUP GATEWAY UTILITY	TANDEM	Bank Fails	2708	132
PAYMENTS TRANSMISSION SYSTEMS (PTS et al)	IBM MF	Bank Fails	1033	198
VFEA	IBM MF	Bank Fails	99	N/A
UKB CLEARING – DSC PHASE II	Various	Bank Fails		3816
MISTRAL	IBM MF	Bank Fails	1831	N/A
UKB CLEARING – DEBIT IN	IBM MF	Bank Fails	2190	212
UKB CLEARING – CREDIT IN	UNISYS	Bank Fails	340	212
POWER CUSTOMER INFORMATION	IBM MF	Bank Fails	290	N/A
UKB MAINSTREAM	UNISYS	Bank Fails		3722
MIDLAND MONTAGU TRADE FINANCE/ EXPORT FINANCE	IBM AS400	Major Loss	33377	N/A
FOREIGN EXCHANGE	IBM MF	Major Loss	1095	N/A
CREDIT RISK (BLS & CLAS)	IBM MF	Major Loss	459	N/A
ORBIT – MMCB	DEC	Major Loss	430	N/A
SAMUEL MONTAGU SYSTEM	TANDEM	Major Loss	1600	N/A
MAIN LEDGER SYSTEM	IBM MF	Major Loss	46	N/A
POWER ACCOUNTING	IBM MF	Major Loss		N/A
SPECIALISED TRADING	PCs	Major Loss		N/A
OTHER CUSTOMER DATABASES (CBU & CLU)	IBM MF	Major Loss	1160	N/A
DOCUMENTARY TRADE SERVICES	IBM MF	Major Loss	131	N/A
HEXAGON CASH MANAGEMENT – BANKTRAK	IBM MF	Major Loss	320	N/A
CUSTOMER ACCOUNTING (CAS & TAS)	IBM MF	Major Loss	93	N/A
SUPERDORIS	DEC	Major Loss	982	N/A
CORPORATE CUSTOMER INFORMATION SYSTEM	IBM MF	Major Loss		N/A
UKB CLEARING – DSC PHASE I – OUT CLEARING	Various	Major Loss	326	N/A
TELEPATH	PC	Major Loss		N/A
MANAGEMENT ACCOUNTING SYSTEM	IBM 38	Inconvenience	371	N/A
GROUP CORPORATE REPORTING SYSTEM	DEC	Inconvenience		N/A
CORRESPONDENT BANKING SYSTEMS	DEC	N/A		

BUSINESS QUALITY — FUNCTION | VALUE
(Function: Unacceptable, Minor Reservations, Major Reservations, Acceptable, N/A; Value: Cheap, Good Value, Reasonable, Expensive, Exorbitant)

TECHNICAL QUALITY — FUNCTION | PERFORMANCE
(Function: Unacceptable, Minor Reservations, Major Reservations, Acceptable, N/A; Performance: Excellent, Good, Adequate, Poor, Unacceptable)

IT COST £'000s scale: 0, 2,000, 4,000, 6,000, 8,000

Figure 3

MM CORPORATE

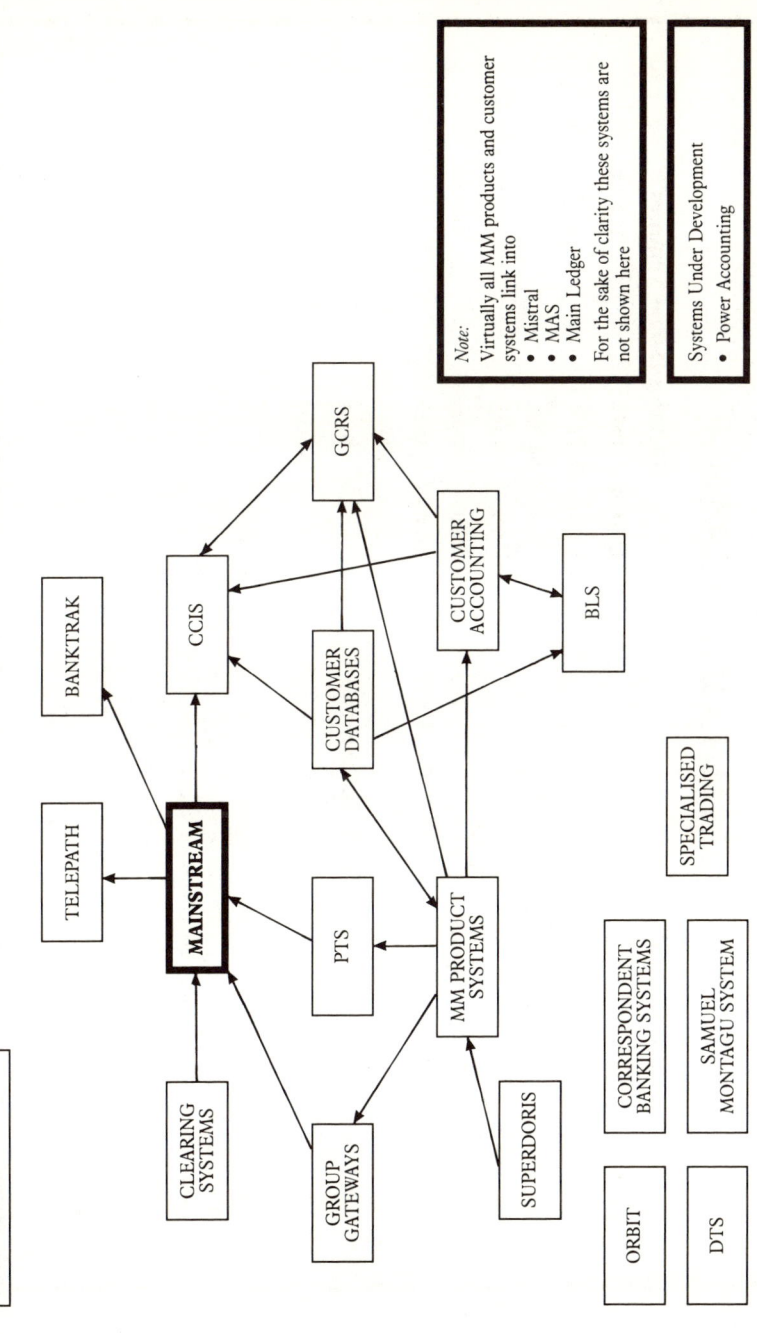

Note:
Virtually all MM products and customer systems link into
- Mistral
- MAS
- Main Ledger

For the sake of clarity these systems are not shown here

Systems Under Development
- Power Accounting

GCRS

BANKTRAK

CCIS

CUSTOMER ACCOUNTING

BLS

CUSTOMER DATABASES

TELEPATH

MAINSTREAM

PTS

MM PRODUCT SYSTEMS

SPECIALISED TRADING

CLEARING SYSTEMS

GROUP GATEWAYS

SUPERDORIS

CORRESPONDENT BANKING SYSTEMS

SAMUEL MONTAGU SYSTEM

ORBIT

DTS

Figure 4

MM CORPORATE

Architectural Issues

Applications Systems

- Multiple accounting systems for Corporates
- Customer systems with overlapping functions
- Risk Management systems with overlapping functions
- Incomplete and inconsistent Customer vision
- Complexity of feeds to Banktrak
- Inability to view consolidated customer credit risk position
- Incomplete Globalisation
- Inconsistency between internal (CCIS) and external (Banktrak) views of customers

Data

- Duplicate customer data
- Duplicate risk data
- Inconsistent and incomplete customer data between and within sectors
- No universal Customer identifier implemented

Technology

- ORBIT on DEC

Business Driver Volumes

Driver	Volume
Customer Base	— PCIS 95k
Product Range	— 200+
Price Variations	— 000's per day
Limit Structures	— Many 000's
Transactions/Deals	per day
FX	— 4k
VFEA	— 4k
MMkt	— 6k
Specialised	— 6k
PTS	— 50k

Figure 5

92

When the Group IT Board considers the proposed overall IT plan (annually just before budgets are set), they address the following four major questions:

1. Is the total plan affordable?

■ Midland's annual spend on IT is typically between £350m-£400m, therefore it is around 18% of non-interest expense (NIE) (this percentage is within the norm for major money centre/clearing banks). They need to relate the overall levels of expenditure and the main components of that expenditure such as staff and equipment. They consider the general trends and the changes of mix of the total expenditure. The relative proportions of expenditure on development and maintenance are also assessed.

■ All this is considered against the background of the overall Group environment; its plans for controlling total costs versus the part that IT can play by helping to reduce costs further in other parts of the Group; the short-term pressures versus the long-term needs.

■ Figures 6 and 7 *(see pages 94-95)* are examples of the analysis work undertaken.

2. Are we investing in the right business areas?

■ The major recipients of IT investment should be those SBUs producing the highest return on equity (ROE) or those whose ROE performance could be transformed by greater investment in IT.

3. Is the investment targeted at the best opportunities?

■ Are we planning to do the right things in those selected SBUs? eg:
   ● Cost Saving: allowing the same tasks to be performed more cheaply produces an improved ROE.
   ● Income Generation: providing new products or opportunities will allow the business to grow.
   ● Information Provision: through the efficient collection and presentation of information we can manage our operations more effectively.

4. Is our IT expenditure being managed well?

■ With IT costs such a significant % of NIE it is very important

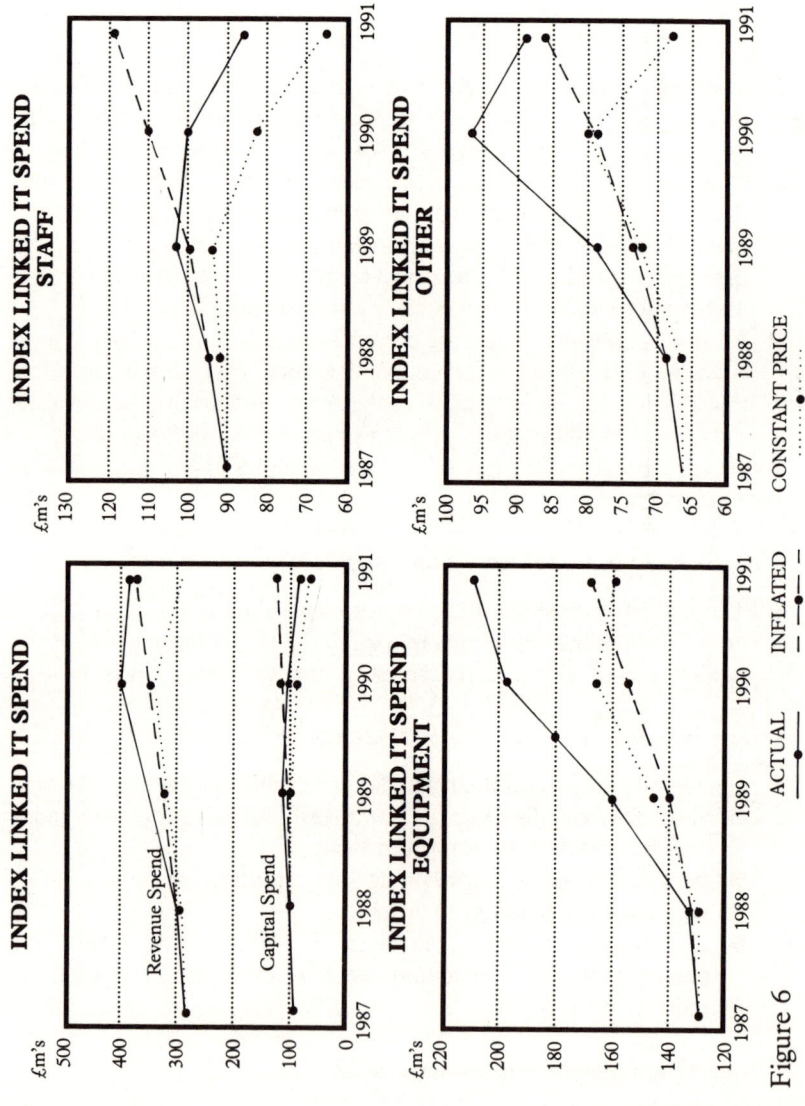

Figure 6

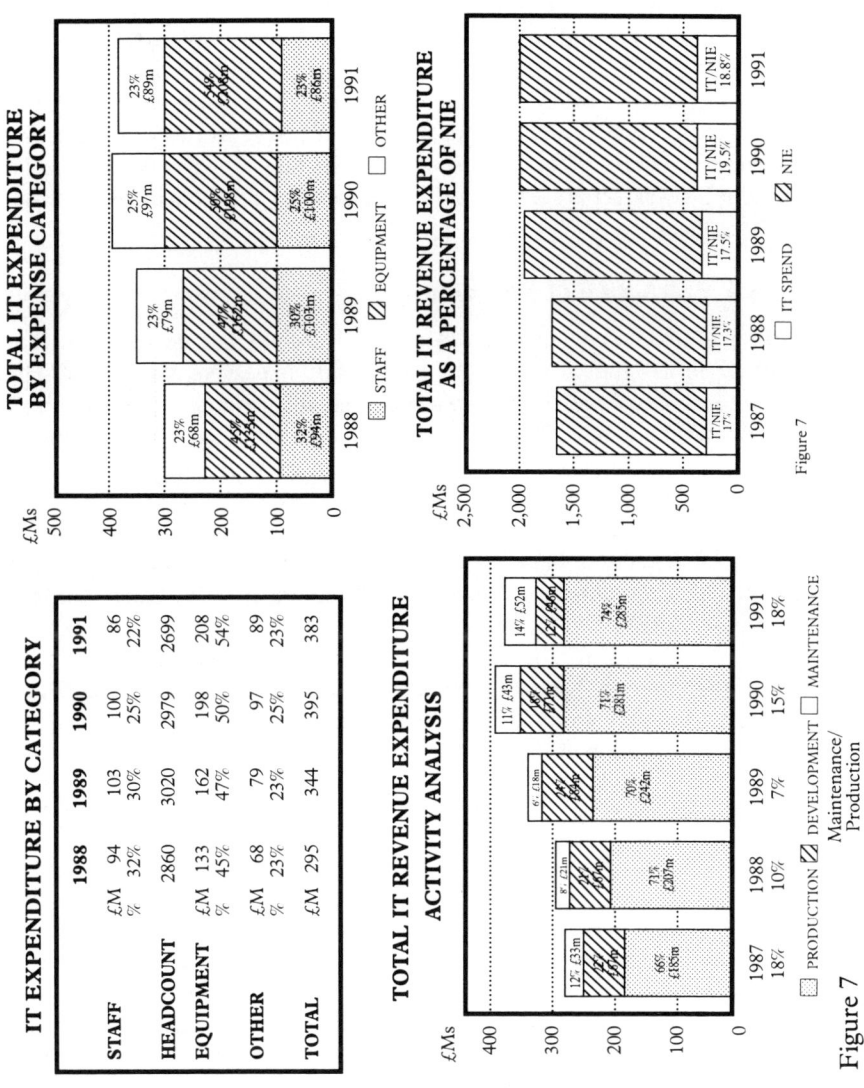

TOTAL IT EXPENDITURE BY EXPENSE CATEGORY

IT EXPENDITURE BY CATEGORY

TOTAL IT REVENUE EXPENDITURE AS A PERCENTAGE OF NIE

TOTAL IT REVENUE EXPENDITURE ACTIVITY ANALYSIS

Figure 7

95

that the whole function is managed professionally. Section 4 of this paper discusses this more fully.

Questions 1-3 are about **effectiveness** (doing the right job) and question 4 is about **efficiency** (doing the job right).

Experience indicates clearly that technology planning is more successful if it is business-driven. Surveys amongst the leading US banks show that in 77% of instances, where IT projects were viewed as successful, IT Planning was part of the business strategy or driven by business needs. 61% of unsuccessful instances occurred when IT Planning was separated from the business or only undertaken on an *ad-hoc* basis.

2.3 A Pro-Active IT Function

Having advocated business-led plans, it should not be assumed that the IT professionals' role in the partnership is passive, far from it. The *true* IT professional should always be business-oriented, but capable of thinking about how IT can be enhanced to add even greater value to the business. Appendices I and II give two examples to show the type of thinking that should be coming from a pro-active IT function, and which have real relevance to all our operations today, in an increasingly IT-dependent banking industry.

The first example (Appendix I) depicts how business strategy thinking and IT strategy thinking *have* to move in unison. The second example (Appendix II) describes two new developments in the IT world (Electronic Data Interchange and Document Image Processing), which are likely to have major effects on our banking industry. Pro-active IT thinking of this nature will help a bank to stay in front.

2.4 Summary

Although most banks and financial institutions accept that they need a strategy for IT, many regard the task as a chore that is the exclusive province of the systems department. But a genuinely strategic direction for IT reflects the organisation's needs to involve business managers as well as IT staff from an early stage. Methodologies are useful, but not enough to ensure ongoing commitment and achievement of the goals set. Only when IT is regarded as a "natural" and integral part of a bank will IT strategy planning no longer be regarded as a one-off task or chore, but more an essential and ongoing element in business strategy planning.

3. Managing the Efficiency of IT

Managing the IT function in any bank requires well-developed professionalism. In Midland, IT divides basically into three types of activity:

- Planning and Architecture
- Systems
- Operations

However, there is an additional dimension to the efficiency of IT which needs to be managed with considerable skill and which is not always recognised by financial institutions:

- IT Vendors

The management of each of these is covered in turn.

3.1 Planning and Architecture

A pro-active IT Planning and Architecture function should:

- be capable of "tuning in" to the business planners;
- help the business planners by suggesting ways in which IT can add further value to the business;
- be the custodians of the overall IT plan; and
- link all this to what is currently being done and ensure there is a clear direction for IT across the whole bank, with architectural visions which do not expose the business to undue technical risk and yet obtain competitive edge from IT wherever possible.

It is a difficult balancing act, but so essential to get right.

3.2 Systems

In the systems area there are four Key Result Areas (KRAs) which are fundamental to ensuring the bank is supported:

1. Ensuring that the IT Solutions Meet the Real Business Need

- This requires systems people to be alert and pro-active, especially during the early analytical phases. Sometimes the apparent problem for which the project was started turns out not to be the *root* cause or requirement.

2. Delivering on Time

- When IT systems people are commissioned to undertake a project

97

and quote timescales for delivering the results, it is important they feel they're entering into a *contract* with their users, who are in effect their customers.

■ This implies that quoted timescales are arrived at responsibly, and then systems people work hard at delivering even earlier. It makes sense to "front-end load" a project to create space to deal with the unforeseen problems which will inevitably occur.

■ A wise project manager will have calculated contingency into the timescale and then "lock it away" for use only in emergencies, rather than be divided up for each part of the project to use up as required. Any gains in any part of the project are also banked and added onto the contingency.

■ Systems people should be stuck with the firm commitment they *first* make as far as the user is concerned. If a project hits problems and is replanned, it is not the replanned date the user remembers.

3. Delivery within Budget

■ The same comments and principles apply for money as for timescale.

4. Build in Quality and Reliability

■ The life of a major banking system usually runs for a long time — often 15-20 years. Once delivered, the costs of production over its life far outweigh the development costs. It is easy to see, therefore, why quality and reliability are so important.

■ This means a newly-developed system should be:
  ● thoroughly tested so the system goes "live" free from significant problems;
  ● reliable well into its production life;
  ● able to conform to the organisation's technical standards;
  ● easy to maintain;
  ● easy to recover, in the event of problems being encountered when it is in production, and not involving protracted recovery procedures. This is very important where there are systems which feed others and when "overnight windows" are very tight and cannot afford lengthy recoveries; and
  ● running at a cost similar to those given in the original business case on which the decision was made. The consumed amount of computing power, storage and telecommunications network are all part of the success measurement for this particular KRA.

If systems designers deliver against these four fundamental KRAs every time, or even 95% of the time, then they will be in true partnership with the business.

3.3 Operations

IT Operations is not a support function but a "sharp-end" production activity and very much a part of banking these days, through the provision of on-line, real-time systems which are often directly accessed by customers. Thus the impact that IT Operations has on customer perceptions can be very significant. Today, we do hear of customers taking their business away to other banks if the computer operations are not giving good service.

There are three basic KRAs for IT Operations:

1. Deliver to Service Quality Targets

■ In Midland there are Service Level Agreements (SLAs) agreed with the Users for each system which is run — and there are about 150 systems run daily! The SLAs define the level of service to be provided for users at the terminal. The key measures here are:
  ● terminal-hour availability
  ● response times when connected.
■ It is no longer relevant to measure performance as the percentage of total time available for the system on the mainframe computer — which has been the traditional method. This has ignored network performance and local hardware performance (eg terminals and terminal servers). Midland have introduced new tools to measure automatically service experienced at the terminal — whether it is a keyboard used by a dealer or back-office clerk, or whether it is a cash machine used by a customer.

2. Reduce Unit Costs

■ The basic measures of unit costs are:
  ● cost per unit of computing power (m.i.p.s. †);
  ● cost per unit of data storage (gigabytes);
  ● cost per item transmitted over the data network.
■ These costs are influenced by:
  ● maximising the economies of scale;

† millions of instructions per second

99

- utilising to a high level the equipment already in use before purchasing further capacity;
- having the right tools to extract as much as possible from automation for the running of computer centres and data networks, so as to contain manpower costs.

■ Midland adopted a Data Centre Strategy in 1987 which used this "utility" approach. It did so because we realised we were spending over £100m per annum on a highly centralised approach, with:

- 30 different data centres housing over 100 different computers;
- data centre premises occupying 450,000 square feet of "raised floor" space;
- 13 different makes of computer on incompatible technologies;
- 1500 people involved in running them; and
- a potential future compound growth rate of 30% per annum.

■ By adopting a *Utility* approach we have:

- reduced the number of data centres to three plus a very few small local processing sites;
- reduced the staff by 40% in four years;
- reduced the makes of computer to five;
- reduced costs in real terms by 24%;
- reduced unit costs every year since 1987;
- handled 2.5 times the volume of work; and
- successfully implemented a Data Centre Strategy in four years, which will save the Midland Group £200m in under 10 years!

3. Being Responsive to Business Demand

■ IT Operations often have to find ways of delivering new services, or extensions of existing services, with little notice of demand and often outside the plan. This of course can put at risk the other KRAs of reducing unit cost and delivering high quality service when something extra has to be fitted in, as well as handling all the things which *are* in plan.

■ It just has to be done! With the competition for business getting tougher all the time, Operations just have to be supportive and find ways of meeting the extra demand. It places even greater emphasis on the need for IT to be close to the business so as to get as much early warning as possible.

100

3.4 IT Vendors

Selecting the right IT Vendors is a very key factor in having an effective IT function in any bank. History is strewn with experience of banks which have been let down by the very vendors on whom they were relying to deliver new capabilities.

Midland have developed this IT area carefully over the last five years and have gained considerable value from it.

The major aims an organisation has to have are to:

- select strategic vendors carefully;
- organise internally to handle vendor relationships;
- recognise that managing vendors carries a cost;
- establish ground rules with vendors about how they conduct their relationship within the customer organisation — very important;
- have a technical strategy to communicate to them — it saves time;
- ensure a single purchasing interface to vendors — this avoids confusion on both sides; and
- learn to say "no" to many of their overtures — we can't be nice all the time!

What Midland require from Strategic Vendors

We have identified who are our strategic vendors and advised each of them that we expect them to:

- take the long view; do not be in a hurry to sell equipment at every opportunity; support us in achieving our main KRAs of reducing cost and delivering service quality;
- support the "utility approach" by working with us on:
  - capacity planning and utilisation
  - automated tools for managing "end-to-end" performance
  - automating operations tasks
  - systems management functions
  - data storage management
  - operating data centres remotely from a single point of control;
- protect our existing investment when announcing new models; we will only replace if it is commercially attractive to us; this requires creative financing/pricing by the vendors;
- provide the right level of support at all levels in our IT organisation;
- ensure we are visible at vendor headquarters; and
- deliver the right commercial terms.

101

In undertaking this approach with vendors we have the following advice for others who may follow a similar approach:

- Rationalise/reduce the number of vendors and decide who is actually "strategic".
- Competition encourages flexibility — even the largest vendor can be flexible when faced with competition!
- Vendors use "divide and conquer" techniques — we work hard at not letting them do that.
- Understand how vendors are organised and how they operate; you will get more from them that way.
- Insist on having a say in the selection of your Account Executive in the vendor team; if you cannot work with him/her then there's no sense in the appointment.
- For specific initiatives, build joint vendor/customer teams with shared objectives.
- Get the highest level of sponsorship with the vendor organisation by having the relationship owned at vendor board level by a specific vendor executive director — when you need to get tough it pays to have someone at that level to whom you can turn.

4. "Staying in Front"

If a bank has put a major effort into achieving an IT function that is both in tune with the business and also managed quite efficiently, then that is not enough. It has to work harder to stay out in front, especially in the current cold climate.

4.1 Managing IT in a Cold Climate

Midland is a major banking and financial services group. Like many other corporations in its field it has been under intense competitive and commercial pressure in recent years.

Under these circumstances the IT function has had to adjust dramatically to the changed climate, both in terms of cutting costs and in being more responsive to those systems opportunities that can have a real impact on the business.

The keys to the approach come down to firstly, breaking the mind-set, so that people do not just keep on working in the same old way when circumstances have changed; secondly, having the right mechanism for recognising and prioritising opportunities for new developments, so that only the really essential ones get approved.

"Breaking the Mind-Set"

One of the problems any organisation faces in adjusting to a dramatically changed climate, or to a different way of working, is that of breaking the mind-set: provoking the necessary degree of change in outlook. Unless and until this is done, people simply tinker with the existing way of doing things. Asked to review a budget, for example, they come back with two per cent or three per cent knocked off, and a view that it would be impossible to do any more without the world collapsing.

Midland took an interesting line on this. The director responsible for IT got his senior management team together and asked how they felt about the total spend of the corporation on IT in the current climate. The figure was about £400m. What, given the needs and financial health of the business, he asked, would seem to them to be the sort of figure that the company ought to spend? Each manager wrote down a number independently. They were surprisingly close. The average came out to be £320m.

Then he asked a second question. If our lives depended on it, could we deliver our services for that figure, without seriously impairing what we currently do for the business? Or put another way, if the IT function was an independent company and we ran out of cash at a spend of £320m, could we find a way of staving off disaster and staying in business?

He then convened a brainstorming session with the team. It had just one rule: "there is no such thing as a silly idea". Anything could be put forward for consideration, nothing was sacrosanct. The first pass produced a number of ideas that were, after discussion, filtered down to a shortlist of practical possibilities. Their total impact amounted to a potential saving of £140m.

"If only half of them prove worth pursuing, we can considerably reduce costs to the extent that would have a significant impact on the group's bottom line. But more than that: we have broken the mind-set. Breakthrough!"

The problem is that without this change in thinking, the issues just cannot be addressed on the right scale.

The cost performance in our Data Centre area, described earlier in Section 4, is an example of what has been achieved.

Staff cuts have also been made — and continue to be made — in the systems development area and in business administration. The effect on morale? No one likes to see cuts, but the overall effect is positive. People can see that we are tackling the problem: we are not simply lying back and letting the business drift along in this climate. We are actually proud of the fact that in some areas, such as the IT planning and architecture groups, we have been able to cut numbers and cost, by 40%. Most IT directors would boast of the numbers they employ!

It is not just a matter of making cuts. Every avenue has to be explored for saving money or getting better value. External services have been reviewed and contracts renegotiated. Outsourcing is under consideration.

Prioritising Development Opportunities

Given tight constraint on overall resources, competition between projects and a wish to put resources on to those projects which have most impact on the business, there is a need for a clear mechanism for evaluating opportunities.

Moreover, within that mechanism, the criteria for the evaluation process need to reflect the current business climate. A project may have an excellent case in terms of cost-return but simply be unaffordable. Or a project may have a high payback when the business actually wants a fast payback.

Midland has adopted a very clear-cut and structured approach to this problem. It focuses on two things: the project's degree of financial attractiveness and whether it is targeted on the right business area.

The "right" business area is one that is already delivering a high performance, based on return on equity — or one that could be substantially moved up the performance table if the proposed system were developed and installed.

The "degree of financial attractiveness" is a factored rating based on such items as internal rate of return, payback period, overall size of payback and risk.

These two considerations can be set out on a "priority matrix", against which proposed projects can be plotted and compared:

(See next page)

104

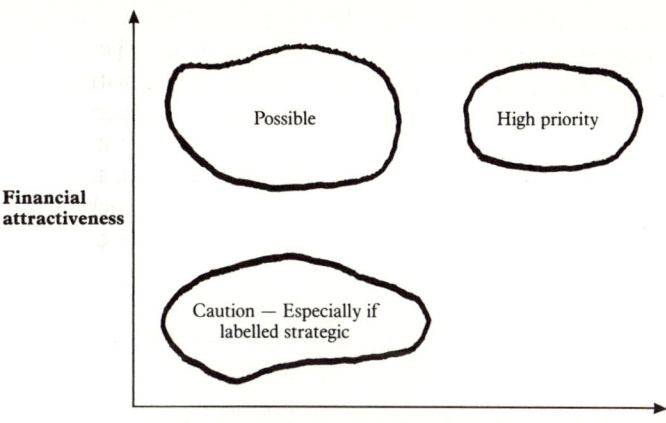

Possible

High priority

**Financial
attractiveness**

Caution — Especially if
labelled strategic

Business units (rated by ROE performance)

Every new development has to have a business sponsor who has to argue the case for the project and who takes subsequent responsibility for the delivery of the business benefits.

Overall Midland has adopted a very clear, some might say hard-nosed, approach to controlling IT in a tough business climate. The very least that could be said for the approach is that it is completely in line with the needs and the mood of the business.

4.2 People Management and Development

Midland has over 2500 people working in IT. "Staying in Front" means that a workforce of that size needs careful management and development — it is a KRA for the IT Directors. Here are extracts of the objectives for senior executives managing the IT function.

KRA — People Management and Development

Objective	*How Success Judged*
(a) Continue to identify and develop key people	■ Existence of "top 200" list with actions for development identified
	■ Implementation of agreed actions for 50% of "top 200"
	■ Put various groups through the targeted levels of training

105

(b) Identify management development plan for all senior management and other management positions

- IT Policy Committee produce/approve an agreed plan
- Updated at least annually

(c) Ensure that a co-ordinated Group IT integrated graduate recruitment and development programme covering 1990 entrants and 1991 recruits

- To satisfaction of IT Policy Committee

(d) Improve productivity of IT staff

- Specific measures to be agreed for each major group of staff, targets identified and then monitored

(e) Encourage a culture of "local" accountability

- When managers begin to manage cost (& profit) centres as if it were their own money at stake

(f) Continue teamwork across Group IT

- Effectiveness of IT Policy Committee
- Support for each other
- Lack of politics

(g) Ensure objectives are set for management of all divisions and formal mid-year feedback on performance is given to all managers

- When they are consistent with agreed Group KRAs and objectives
- Planned objectives and strategic developments widely understood and accepted
- When objectives are met
- When performance ratings and performance-related pay are consistently applied across Group IT

(h) Monitor morale

- Staff turnover & absenteeism not to exceed market norm in each area
- Employee attitude surveys

- Sensitive management of change
- Grievances & disciplinary hearings are at an acceptable level

4.3 Working at Communications

If the IT population is to be motivated to give its best, then it is important that they are told what is going on, feel they are able to voice opinions to senior management, see that IT management are visible and "walk the talk".

In Midland we lay heavy emphasis on our managers being good at communicating, and IT is no different in this respect. Again, it is a KRA. Listed below are typical objectives that each senior manager in IT has for communications.

KRA — Communications

Objective	*How Success Judged*
(a) Through positive leadership, establish confidence and belief of management, staff and customers in Midland's success	■ When major areas of Group IT give positive feedback during visits "Sevens" † lunches, etc.
(b) Communicate Key Group IT roles, directions, strategies and progress	■ When all Group IT areas give positive feedback ■ When other parts of the Group understand basic messages about direction of Group IT
(c) Build and continue to re-inforce the partnership concept with major users	■ SBUs view Group IT as supportive to their businesses and successfully adding value
(d) Senior management regularly visit to departments in Group IT and User areas	■ When Group IT senior management is regarded as in touch with people across many areas and at different levels
(e) Continue to improve the focus on existing practices of all line areas and encourage/ achieve ownership of communications issues	■ When line management across Group IT are viewed by staff as good at communications ● favourable feedback received

- When line management is visible through regular contact/ meetings with:
  - Management and staff
  - Unions
  - Users
- When major developments in the Group are talked about and understood
- When "Sevens"† lunches are perceived as useful opportunities to meet and exchange views and ideas

5. Conclusion

Banking and Information Technology have made considerable progress together over the past 20 years and should now have reached a "mature" relationship. However, the challenge of the next 10 years is so great for the banking industry, with IT playing such a key role, that we have to re-examine whether that relationship is sufficiently well-developed to meet that challenge.

As the business and technology become more intertwined, we find that business management needs IT awareness (if not skills) and vice-versa.

This paper has attempted to show how "The Technology Response" to the business might be handled. Clearly each bank is unique in many respects, but I hope there is enough "core thinking" in the views expressed here which can be adapted to suit individual organisations' needs.

---

† A "Sevens" lunch is a communications forum whereby executive management exchange views with managers from departments and branches across Midland Group.

Appendix I

"Customer or Product"

In order to develop a *vision* of a bank's business strategy with a view to guiding systems architecture, we should consider whether a *product-based* or a *customer-based* focus should predominate; we should also consider whether these focuses should carry "equal" weight or some combination thereof.

1. Terminology

"What do we mean by a product-based and a customer-based business?"

In a product-based business the principal economic proposition is the idea that one product or group of products (product family) forms the basis of a business and can generate identifiable revenues, costs and profits. There is also the notion that the business line is, relatively speaking, "stand-alone" or can exist substantially in isolation from other related businesses. Of course, a product-based business has *customers* and may segment its marketplace to tailor its service propositions to different groups of customers. Nevertheless, it sees its primary mission as to deliver a single product or a product family to *many* customers.

A customer-based business places the emphasis the other way round. Its mission is to supply many products and product families to a single *customer* or, more likely, to a *group of customers* who form a market segment with many common characteristics. In a customer-based business there may be a number of "core products" around which the profit equation broadly coalesces, with the sale of additional products offering further profit enhancement opportunities.

2. Application to Banking

"Banking started with customers but became progressively more product-driven."

Money and financial service businesses offer many points of linkage and exhibit a high degree of substitution. Accordingly, a banking institution succeeds in profit terms by orchestrating a number of linked service propositions to its customer base, in order to create a "virtuous circle" of profit growth off a given customer franchise.

In this sense it differs from many manufacturing and other service industries where products are well defined and where linkages are less obvious. Nevertheless, in some consulting and engineering areas in certain well integrated areas of manufacturing, and in some fields such as transportation, the same linkage opportunities arise. It is arguable that maximising the cross-sale of products is one of the *key* management challenges in banking.

If one takes a historical perspective, it is fair to say that banking started as a customer-based business, albeit that the range of products was generally limited to a "core" group, such as moving money and intermediating between "borrowers" and "lenders". Because credit was essentially very short-term in nature (eg overdrafts and discounting bills of exchange), it was not easily possible to separate money transmission and credit provision. This came later as technology came to bear on the basic money transmission function and banking moved into longer-term and more discrete forms of credit extension.

At the same time, banks developed specialist services, eg leasing, foreign exchange, capital markets and credit cards, which were almost always organised on *product-based* lines, even though they attempted to access the "core" customer base of the whole banking institution. Further developments produced the famous "relationship banking" philosophy (customer-based), which contrasted somewhat tritely and even uneasily with the "transaction" banking beloved of investment banks and those who emulated them.

The swings in sentiment towards these two apparently opposite styles produced a fair degree of organisational disharmony in many banks, and illustrate the previous point about how complex and yet how fruitful a solution to these issues can be for profitable business development.

3. Application to ABC Bank

"ABC Bank exhibits both customer-based and product-based business models and some mixtures."

Examples of customer-based and product-based approaches to various group businesses can be cited. Further examples can be cited where frankly it is not clear what the guiding organisational principle is.

Customer-based Businesses:

- Branch banking for Retail and Enterprise Customers;
- Middle Market Corporates Banking;
- Major Corporates Banking;
- Correspondent Banking;
- Private Banking.

Product-based Businesses:

- Treasury & Capital Markets;
- Securities and Global Custody Services;
- Trade & Project Finance;
- Asset Management;
- Leasing & Factoring;
- Newer approaches to retail banking products, eg direct banking and mortgage lending.

Mixed Businesses:

- Electronic banking and money transmission;
- Cards;
- Corporate and specialised finance.

Are they a businesses or a utility product? The answer must vary.

Relationship banking has taken hold in ABC Bank over the last 10 years. It is fair to say that the relationship managers tend to concentrate on a group of core products, particularly in money transmission and basic lending. Nevertheless, a true understanding of the nature of the revenue, costs and profits streams generated by these customer-based commercial banking businesses is still weak and largely confined to measures of activity thrown up by the product processing systems, which serve these core product families.

Many of the pure product-based businesses, on the other hand, have higher levels of product profitability information.

4. Possible Conclusions

- The cost and ultimate benefit of managing too many customer-based businesses may outweigh the benefits. Measurement is already a difficult task and it could become unmanageable. Relationship managers may be better off concentrating on a narrow range of "core" products for which measurement systems can be developed and relying on "referral" points for other products.

■ There is no doubt that for many correspondent banks and corporate customers, the concept of "relationship" and relationship profitability is a *reality* and should be catered for in information systems terms. For example, a money transmission relationship usually requires a core borrowing facility.

■ On the other hand, more products than is commonly thought could be the subject of a product-based approach. This may help to simplify our business and the required systems support to a significant degree.

■ Some products are not really discrete products but "utilities", which support other products or activities, eg electronic banking, high-value payment systems and some applications of cards.

■ A bank needs to explore ways of processing the same products in the same systems, rather than having different systems developed for an internal organisational sector.

■ A review of current systems architecture is needed to attempt to catalogue the systems used to support all a bank's businesses. The analysis should break systems down into sales/customer, product processing, distribution and control. This is a convenient way of cataloguing systems in meaningful groups.

The analysis should examine the businesses in terms of a two-dimensional matrix tracking customer segment and product segment. This approach allows one to be *neutral* about which principle is predominant, ie customer or product. However, this analysis alone will suggest the feasibility and desirability of managing each box in the matrix (each one of which can be a business in its own right) either by product or customer or a combination of both. An example of the matrix is in Attachment 1 on page 114 and study of this may clarify the point being made.

A typical box in the matrix might be:

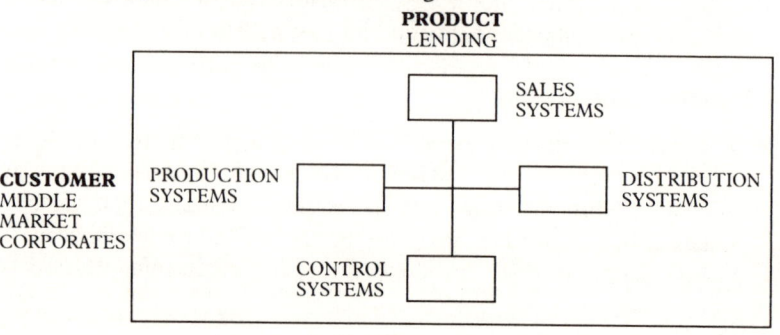

PRODUCT
LENDING

SALES SYSTEMS

CUSTOMER MIDDLE MARKET CORPORATES

PRODUCTION SYSTEMS

DISTRIBUTION SYSTEMS

CONTROL SYSTEMS

This box analyses how we support one "business" or "sub-business", namely the provision of core lending products to middle market corporate customers. Systems are then catalogued to highlight duplication and potential for improvement.

Another might be the provision of Treasury services to correspondent banks.

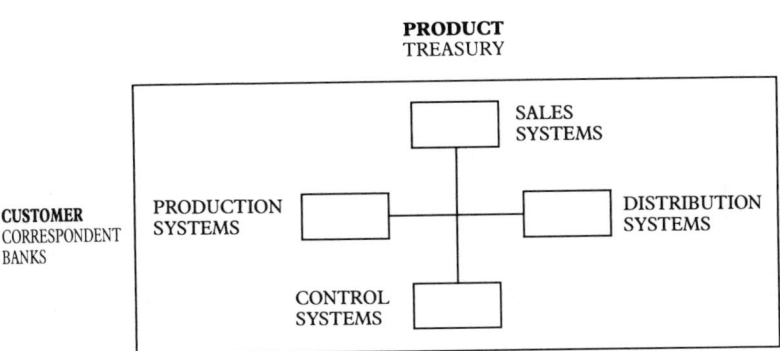

The task is rigorous and time-consuming and there will be a lot of repetition. But it will be exhaustive and allow both the product-based and customer-based view to be taken. Some boxes will be blank. No reference is made to the third dimension, ie geography — for the sake of simplicity.

■ There is no obvious answer to whether a customer-based or a product-based approach should predominate; organisation will shift over time and in response to market forces. However, it is critical to know, *at any point in time,* which of the drivers is being used for a given customer or product segment. This allows product management functions to understand whether they are "subsidiary" or "in command". Of course, management activity and control can, and should be, exercised over both the "rows" and "columns" in the degree to which it is felt necessary. What is certain is that any systems architecture must be flexible and cost-effective enough to handle both product-based and customer-based approaches as clearly determined by senior management.

	'Core' Lending and Credit	Domestic Money Transmission	Classical Intl Trade/ Payments Products	Trade and Project Finance	Treasury and Capital Markets	Corporate Finance and Related	Asset Management	Asset- Based Finance	Custody/ Securities Services	Cards
Retail Customers										
Enterprise Customers										
Middle Market Corporates (UKCB)	P S / D C									
High Net Worth Individuals										
Non-Bank Financial Institutions										
Correspondent Banks					P S / D C					
Large Corporates (MMCB)										

Attachment 1

114

Appendix II

Recent Developments in the IT World
1. Electronic Data Interchange

What is EDI?

EDI stands for Electronic Data Interchange, and is sometimes known as Electronic Trading. It is a method for the sending of messages between the computers of two separate organisations, using widely accepted standards for the content of the messages sent.

By now everyone is familiar with Electronic Mail. This is also a form of electronic messaging, but the content of messages is totally unstructured, and requires interpretation by a person. It is therefore a "person to person" messaging system. EDI on the other hand is the sending of electronic documents between organisations, so structured that the company's computer systems themselves can both construct them for sending out, and interpret them when they arrive.

In a sense, SWIFT (Society for World Interbank Financial Telecommunications) and CHAPS (Clearing Houses Automated Payments System) are EDI systems: but the standards, although widely used, are particular to these applications.

Until 18 months ago, EDI users basically fell into three groups, defined by the standards used. These were:

- users of the INS network TRADANET, which uses the TRADA-COMS standard;
- users of the ISTEL network (now owned by AT&T), which uses the ODETTE standard;
- users who have developed their own standards, either for in-house applications, or as a bipartite agreement between them and some of their trading partners.

Larger corporates dictated to smaller trading partners which standard to follow, locking them into a particular family of users. This partitioning meant that only users on the same EDI network could send EDI messages to one another.

But the very essence of EDI is the adoption of widely accepted standards, and the one that has emerged internationally, sponsored by the United Nations, is EDIFACT. Network providers are increasingly making available EDIFACT as well as their own proprietary standard, and this is fast eliminating the restrictive local standards. A lot of work is being put into considering how the local standards can be migrated

115

to EDIFACT with minimum disruption for users.

Currently in the UK about 4000 corporates are using EDI, and the number is growing at 40% a year. This includes 800 or so smaller companies (turnover less than £20m), although generally the smaller corporate will be involved because of the wishes of a larger trading partner.

The advantages to be gained by EDI arise from avoiding handling paper. This means that costs are reduced (US market research indicates $4.70 for an EDI transaction as against $49 for paper), less errors are made rekeying information, and stock levels can be reduced through responsive just-in-time ordering systems. It may be possible at this time to gain competitive edge through the use of EDI and the faster and more flexible options it offers, but, in the not very distant future, the use of EDI will become the norm in many fields, making it a competitive disadvantage not to offer it as a means of trading with suppliers and customers.

Relationship to Financial Services

Historically, EDI was used to transfer documentation referring to trade, such as the sending of orders for goods, and the invoices. Just-in-time ordering especially requires a fast and responsive ordering system. Increasingly, other types of document are being included, for instance, engineering diagram drawings, architectural drawings, advertising artwork, etc, and, of particular interest, financial information.

It is anticipated that growth in financial EDI applications will "shadow" growth in commercial EDI. Research has shown that corporates require financial EDI services to provide:

■ guaranteed payment dates to corporates. Without this guarantee corporates will be faced with the same uncertainties they currently experience when sending cheques to their trading partners by post. However, many accounts payable managers see these delays, which occur as part of "the cheque's in the post" scenario, as beneficial — putting off when they need to pay. EDI payments will not remove their ability to control when a payment should be made — it will strengthen it by the fact that they *will* know when a payment will be made. The benefit to the corporate treasurer is certain know-ledge of funds available for investment purposes. More enlightened managers recognise that a likely spin-off from such guaranteed value dates is their ability to negotiate better discounts with suppliers on the basis of guaranteed income allowing better cash management. As such, the "benefits" of losing cheques in the top right hand drawer will be superceded by better terms of business negotiated from guaranteed payment dates.

■ guaranteed security in the processing and transmission of payments and accompanying remittance advices. Not surprisingly, people are nervous about making payments electronically. To allay both perceived and real concerns about security, providers of financial EDI services must provide effective security methods. The banks are approaching security in different ways. An example of co-operation between suppliers in addressing the security issues related to financial EDI is the EDI Association's security demonstrator project. This initiative involves two software companies, SD-Scicon and Data Interchange, and two security companies, Zergo and Smart Diskette. Individual smartcards will enable different people in organisations to authorise payments up to different amounts. Digital signatures and the application of EDIFACT security standards will ensure end-to-end security. The security these techniques offer needs to be matched by comparable organisational management. For example, clear payment procedures, authorisation levels and payment timings all need to be agreed and adhered to.

The EDI payments services currently available are limited because they can only handle intra-bank EDI payments. This falls short of the requirements of companies which are looking for an "open payments environment". To address this need was the purpose of an inter-bank payments initiative to develop an EDI clearing capability involving the five major clearing banks (Midland, Lloyds, NatWest, Royal Bank of Scotland and Barclays). This capability will enable the banks offering EDI payment services to pass EDI payments and associated remittance information from their corporate customers to the trading partners via the trading partner's bank. The capability will be run as a pilot for the first six months to a year, and will be available by the end of this year. Settlement will be achieved by CHAPS in the pilot, but this route is expected to be only a tactical solution, with EDI settlement being introduced once a full system is developed.

What Steps should be Taken?

Companies large and small are increasingly beginning to use EDI in order to streamline their operation. These companies will come to favour those trading partners who help them leverage this by agreeing to trade with them using EDI. As suppliers of financial services, the finance industry will need to respond to this demand.

It will be important for financial service providers to enter into a dialogue with their customers, and seek to influence their approach to the adoption of EDI so that they can get the full benefit of a future integrated trade and payment service. Corporates will also be looking to their providers of financial services to provide an easy and secure means of connecting themselves into the financial aspects of such system. It will be important that financial service organisations have a strategy suitable for the various requirements of their differing customers' segments.

2. Document Image Processing

What is Document Image Processing?

Document Image Processing (DIP) refers to the handling and control of scanned documents, and related services such as workflow management, sophisticated document storage, and OCR (Optical Character Recognition).

DIP consists of scanning and storing documents for viewing and manipulation. Typically the document will be scanned at a workstation (often called a Scan Station), and stored in a compressed form on a database of images. This will usually consist of an index database, probably a standard relational database, which will hold all the indices by which the document is to be retrieved, whilst the image itself is physically stored in a separate database.

Optical disc storage is frequently associated with DIP since the images are large, and not generally intended for update. Optical disc storage is not a necessity for DIP, and its use is more a matter of balancing storage cost against required access performance. The storage management concepts being adopted by IBM for example on their large systems would tend to hide the systems choice of media from the user in any case. Optical disc technology is similar to that of CD players. For DIP the discs can be 5¼″ or 12″ discs, in either individual drives or as a library in juke boxes. Juke boxes contain many operator replaceable discs which can be brought on-line to one or more read stations.

A related and in fact much more important aspect of the technology is Case or Workflow Processing, where a "folder" of working documents is held together and submitted to various staff at workstations for action. Workstation operators view the documents on image screens and take whatever action is necessary, assisted by the facilities of the Case Processing system which will include menu-based task control, diarising facilities, automated letter, fax and telex generation etc. As a technology, Case transcends Image since it can deal with any input material, including Electronic Mail or EDI messages, stored voice messages, messages from dp applications or even the original documents. The ultimate aim is for all correspondence to be conducted electronically with no documents to scan.

Workstation operators will frequently wish to take information from a scanned document and input it to a standard data processing application, eg inputting details from an application form. The DIP system can assist this by providing several windows so that the document and the input screen can be viewed together, plus facilities whereby the operator "cuts and pastes" from the input document onto the input screen. All this will generally require wide screens.

For economy of transmission and storage, images are compressed, using various algorithms. The degree of compression depends on various criteria, for instance, both hatched backgrounds and colour affect compression. Other techniques are used to reduce the image size, for instance capturing only the relevant data by trimming off the unwanted areas, or using drop-out ink for form printing. Inks of certain colours cannot be seen by particular scanners and the form is reconstituted at the other end from templates. This means that all workstations accessing the images must adhere to common standards.

There are unresolved legal issues involved in the validity of images as evidence. Best legal advice is that it will be acceptable provided it can be shown that the system is standard practice, incapable of updating the image, or that this is well audited. WORM (Write Once Read Only) optical disc obviously assists here. So most companies who image important legal documents also file them away, albeit in cheap remote locations.

Relevance to Financial Institutions

DIP can be used to save floorspace, typically where there are many documents, needing quick access by several people. Benefits are reductions in premises costs and lost or absent files, and possibly faster response to customer enquiries.

Case or Workflow Processing is however the major application that will deliver real benefit. Customer queries, requests for services, or other correspondence, are entered as they arrive in a post room, and directed by automated routing and supervisor control to particular clerks for processing. A particular case may take a long time (eg a mortgage application, or taking of security) and may also result in legal documents to be archived.

Other applications may involve the holding of images of signature mandates, for use at several locations (eg branches and head office).

Potential cheque processing applications are:

- use of OCR to read the Courtesy Amount on cheques to reduce the human intervention in cheque encoding
- adding an image of the whole cheque to statements, a legal requirement in the US, but as an extra service in the UK

The major barrier to DIP usage is costs, of optical disc (for large storage volumes), of transmitting large volumes of image data, and of software. Although the first two are reducing, all this generally needs to be offset against real cost savings.

What Steps should be Taken?

The importance of Document Image Processing lies very much more in the workflow control offered by Image Processing packages from vendors than the storage of images. This is because the advantages of being able merely to scan and store customers' financial instructions will be eroded by the advent of EDI, telebanking, EftPos and so on.

It is for this reason that it is essential for organisations to understand their operational flow, and to apply the techniques of production engineering to their paper processing, be it centralised or in branches, before embarking on very costly Document Image Processing applications.

This is the ideal time for such an approach to their operations, since the DIP packages being offered by vendors are not mature yet, but are likely to be very credible by the turn of the year. It is important to bear in mind that this kind of system is a radical departure in that it becomes the controller of the institutions operation, not just a tool employed by it. Therefore a clear strategy for operations is a prerequisite for adopting DIP on any scale.

The Ebb and Flow of Japanese International Banking

Dr Andreas R Prindl, FCIB, FCT
Chairman, Nomura Bank International

Dr. Andreas R. Prindl, FCIB, FCT

Andreas R. Prindl was born in 1939. He holds a BA degree in
European languages and literature (Princeton University), an
MA and PhD in international economics (University of
Kentucky) and undertook post-graduate study at the London
School of Economics in 1963-64.

After joining Morgan Guaranty Trust Company of New
York in 1964, he was assigned to Europe where he held a
variety of positions. In 1976, he was transferred to Japan
where he was general manager of Morgan's Tokyo office for
four years. After two years on secondment as chief executive
of Saudi International Bank in London, he then headed the
Morgan Bank mergers and acquisitions team in the U.K. In
1984, Dr. Prindl joined Nomura International Limited as
managing director. He is now Chairman of Nomura Bank
International plc, which he founded in November 1986.

Dr. Prindl has published extensively on a variety of
topics, particularly on changes in the Japanese financial
system and on treasury management.

Contents

Introduction

This paper is about forces and flows, phenomena which shape bankers' strategies. Different currents, emanating from financial, economic and political changes, lead bankers to concentrate on domestic activities, to expand abroad, or to retreat back to a home base. This study, which is based purely on my private opinions, focuses on the Japanese banks. Their international expansion has been recent, rapid and massive; it is also, at the point of writing, ebbing back towards Japan. Much of this movement is a function of the large financial flows which the Japanese houses intermediate, flows which have made the Japanese banks the largest in the world. Analysing such factors may explain the apparent reversal of what looked like an inexorable wave, and threat, just a few years ago.

Such forces and flows, of course, affect large banks in every country. The Japanese example is a particularly vivid one, but is paralleled — over a longer period — by American banks, whose current direction is also away from international penetration, navigating towards more predictable home waters.

To put Japanese banking into context, and to be able to surmise where it may eventually be heading, it is useful to start with a very brief sketch of the past and present Japanese financial system.

1. The Traditional Structure of Japanese Finance

One force which shapes every banking system is the role and policy of its government, passive or active. In Japan's case, its banks were used as a direct and compliant tool of government economic policy over many years.

The historic role of Japanese financial institutions was to support the growth of the Japanese economy by efficiently channelling domestic savings to government-sponsored industrial channels, under Ministry of Finance and Bank of Japan control. Especially since World War II, there has been state planning for industry, including state direction of finance. Japanese banks were given the strongest possible *guidance* to lend to selected borrowers or sectors, even down to individual quotas for lending by month and by industry. Interest rates on both deposits and loans were set by government, often at artificially low levels. Given the enormous task of redeveloping Japan after the devastation of World War II, such state guidance was not only necessary, but also consonant with the structure of Japanese society. This

125

structure is a vertical one, based on strict adherence to authority and direction from abroad. In such a structure, *segmentation* also arises: specific types of institutions are set up to do specific jobs. A quite differentiated financial system arose, even before the war. Americans imposed a variety of habits upon Japan during the occupation; the US Glass-Steagall separation of banking and securities was ensconced in Article 65 of the Japanese Securities and Exchange Law as a similar barrier.

During most of the 20th century, therefore, the Japanese financial system has operated with a number of different types of financial institution, each with its own legal framework and clearly delineated area of operations. These include 13 "city banks" (like British clearers), seven trust banks, three long-term banks, a host of regional, co-operative and agricultural banks, and a very strong securities sector, headed by four industry leaders. The city banks took deposits and lent directly to industry for working capital, but could not issue their own bonds. Banks with a longer-term orientation could issue publicly, and were the main instrument of the Japanese government in fostering the growth of heavy industry, then consumer goods/export orientated companies, then high technology. The securities companies followed the same national policy in shaping both primary and secondary securities markets towards efficient industrial finance. Their role sharply increased when the Japanese government developed big public sector borrowing requirements in the mid-1970s after the first oil shock.

All Japanese financial houses were subject to the direction of the Ministry of Finance, under three main bureaux: Banking, Securities and International Finance. The banks were subject to tight Bank of Japan guidance as well. The bureaux regulated, but also looked out for, the interests of their respective houses: the increasingly intense competition between banks and securities houses is mirrored at the Ministry of Finance.

That this Ministry and the Bank of Japan were able to direct with little demur the Japanese financial system in such detail is an unusual characteristic for an advanced capitalist country. Official guidance could go as far as individual interest rates on individual loans, or detailed instructions to securities houses on timing and price of specific new issues, as well as support of the Tokyo stock market and various listed companies, to a degree unmatched in the West. Indeed, another example of this potentially stifling type of minute state control is communism, not capitalism. But it works in Japan, for several reasons.

Firstly, the role and acceptance of authority are deeply ingrained in Japanese society, as in other Confucian-oriented countries. Vertical responsibility/guidance are paramount and companies or individuals are accustomed to following without question the guidance of their superiors, whether it be the elders of the rice-growing villages from which Japan stems, or their modern parallel, the ministries in Kasumigaseki, especially the Ministries of Finance (MOF) and International Trade and Industry (MITI). The edicts of ministry officials, themselves among the best and brightest of Japanese graduates, are seldom questioned or disobeyed. Secondly, the financial houses were mainly recycling the domestic savings of Japanese households into Japanese industry. Japanese people for several decades have saved striking percentages of their take-home salary: over 20 per cent in many post-war years, still in the high teens now. The modern Japanese have been classic under-consumers; their propensity to save has been skilfully utilised by the government through various mechanisms, including the enormous Postal Savings Bank, to direct savings towards investment and latterly its own borrowing needs.

Industrial financing was mainly indirect, as external funding was obtained from the domestic banks, rather than direct investors. Banks were, and still are, seen as permanent partners, their position almost like that of equity holders, and they expected to extend their loans (and to receive compensating balances or other business) indefinitely. Large gearing resulted, but, in the context of fast growth and implicit partnership, this bothered nobody. Issuance of new equity was limited, owing to the practice of issuing shares at a low nominal value, rather than at much higher market prices. This reinforced the reliance on bank loans or bonds; the latter had to be collateralised for most companies until the mid 1980s. As a result, sophisticated modern financial instruments did not quickly appear, or their importation into Japan was delayed.

Such a centrally directed, segmented and bank-oriented financial system worked well for almost 40 years, including the oil shock period, when Japan needed huge funds from both domestic and foreign sources. Now Japanese industry is mature and rapidly investing abroad. Manufacturing companies are moving a significant part of their industrial capacity offshore, owing to the strong yen and lasting trade frictions. Producing abroad in Britain or Kentucky is a welcome phenomenon, one well suited to increase Western employment and reduce trade frictions. Many Japanese firms are cash rich and increasingly interested in sophisticated money management.

2. The Flood Tide

For a variety of business and structural reasons, therefore, the Japanese financial institutions turned their approach from an inward-looking to a strong outward-looking one about 10 years ago. Their rapid growth abroad paralleled the large increase in Japanese trade surpluses and resultant capital outflows. The intermediary role in handling these flows made the Japanese banks into the largest in the world and brought the Japanese securities companies to the top of the Eurobond tables. Below are outlined the main currents propelling the Japanese houses into our markets.

a) Business Reasons

Following Japanese Firms Abroad

Japanese commercial banks have emulated other institutions in following their domestic clients abroad. Earlier waves of American and European banks set up foreign branches in overseas markets where their main customers were establishing manufacturing and trading subsidiaries, expecting good chances of business. The sharply increasing trend of Japanese direct investment abroad buttresses this motivation. For example, Japanese FDI moved from only $2.8 billion in 1976 to about $50 billion in 1990.

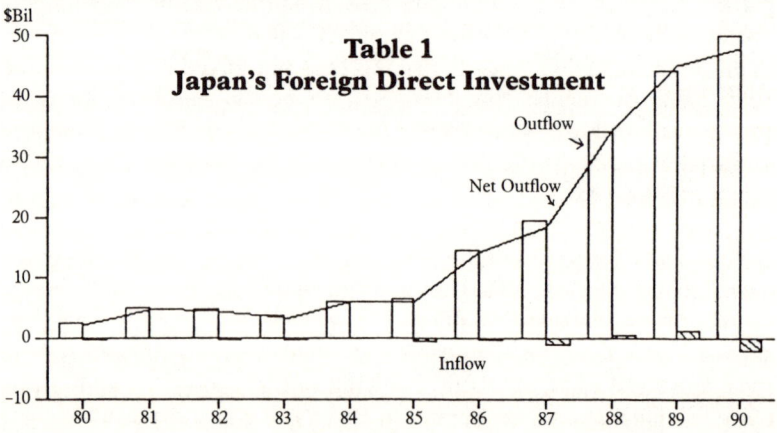

Table 1
Japan's Foreign Direct Investment

128

The 1992 Factor

Without doubt, the 1992 factor will encourage more European direct investment by Japanese companies and banks. Nomura Research Institute believes Japanese investment into Europe will double in 10 years' time from today's level of $9-10 billion per annum. The fear of exclusion from "Fortress Europe" is important; a more positive motive is to be within a huge, continental market where barriers to production, trade and employment are being dismantled. The Common Market approximates the USA in size and buying power and offers much opportunity to strong manufacturing nations like Japan if they are not excluded from this market. Economic growth in Europe is reasonably strong. More production here will lessen Japan's dependence on the US.

Within the EC, the UK is by far the preferred site; it offers a welcoming atmosphere, the presence of successful cases already, such as Sony in Wales and Nissan in north-east England, helped by the position of London as the world's leading financial centre. British labour has turned out to be more efficient and more docile than expected. Even the difficult and splintered British unions have been amenable to long-term or single-union contracts. The UK has so far 24% of the Japanese investment in Europe in number (and far more by value).

Japanese financial houses are responding to the 1992 challenge by setting up local operations in the major financial centres, with local dedicated capital, and converting branches (which could be deemed Japanese) into local companies. They look forward to the increased flexibility of the European Banking Directives, when implemented.

Maturity of the Japanese Home Market

The interest of Japanese banks in directly working with their biggest domestic customers abroad was augmented by the need to find new lending outlets. Sometime in the late 1970s Japan became a mature economic country. Reconstruction after World War II was complete and Japanese industry possessed very modern plants. While infrastructure — roads, parks, sewerage systems, for instance — still leaves much to be desired, the banks have limited opportunity to lend large amounts to non-business sectors. The high savings propensity of the Japanese consumer has not yet allowed a strong retail lending business. Japanese domestic loan demand has fallen since the start of the 1980s, once the dramatic but rapidly overcome effects of the oil shock were over. The need to offset this shortfall in home demand is an important factor in the decision to increase foreign assets. The first attempt at this was simply to lend abroad, especially in the halcyon days of LDC syndications. Since most of that collapsed, direct lending from foreign branches or subsidiaries is a preferred channel.

Entering Areas Closed to them in Japan

The local restrictions of Article 65 are very annoying in the age of *Allfinanz*, but do not apply abroad. Thus, the big Japanese banks and brokers are setting up foreign subsidiaries to gain experience on the opposite side of the regulatory fence. In England, for instance, 22 of the 23 Japanese banks with London operations have investment banking subsidiaries; the four securities houses have set up full-service commercial banks in London with considerable capital and ambitious goals and are obtaining bank licences for several of their European subsidiaries.

The most striking example of this testing the waters was the purchase of majority control of Banca del Gottardo in Lugano by Sumitomo Bank in 1984, the first major acquisition by a Japanese financial house of a European one. Banca del Gottardo is an important institution in the Swiss bond market and possesses excellent under-writing and distribution capabilities. This aggressive move suits the style and image of Sumitomo, typically the most profitable commercial bank in Japan and one which stresses its corporate finance capability in Tokyo. One could also cite Mitsubishi Bank's purchase of Bank of California, as one of several in that State, or the takeover of Walter Heller by Fuji Bank. More typical has been the establishment of those merchant banking/underwriting subsidiaries in London by the major Japanese banks. They are beginning to lead security issues for Japanese issuers (not only from their own *zaibatsu* groupings) and to act as prominent managers and co-managers in issues led by US or European banks.

b) Structural Reasons

Building a Base in the Biggest Markets

Japan is far away, with a non over-lapping time zone; despite liberal-ization, its own capital markets are still relatively small. It is attractive, not only for short-term competitive reasons to be directly involved in larger markets, but also for longer-term structural considerations. At the end of the century there will be fewer international financial institutions in the world — maybe 30 large groups — but they will be much larger. Those institutions will probably cover the waterfront of financial services, including both commercial banking and securities business. The leading survivors will maintain a major foothold in each of the three main world financial centres: London, Tokyo and New York. Putting a base together in London and New York is a long range strategic move in preparation for the globalization and concentration of international finance.

Recycling Japanese Capital Outflows

Japan is now the world's largest capital exporter and this trend is likely to endure. The Japanese trade surplus in 1990 was $63.8 billion. Although down from 1989's $77 billion, this is still higher than the level of Saudi Arabian surpluses at their largest, and more sustainable.

Table 2
Japanese Balance of Payments

($mn)

	1983	1984	1985	1986	1987	1988	1989	1990
Current Account	**20,799**	**35,003**	**49,169**	**85,845**	**87,015**	**79,631**	**57,157**	**35,792**
Long Term Capital	-17,700	-49,651	-64,542	-131,461	-136,532	-130,930	-89,246	-43,455
Portfolio Investments	-1,876	-23,601	-43,032	-101,432	-93,838	-66,651	-28,034	-5,028
Direct Investments	-3,196	-5,975	-5,810	-14,254	-18,354	-34,695	-45,184	-46,191
Others	-12,628	-20,075	-15,700	-15,775	-24,340	-29,584	-16,028	-7,764
Short Term Capital	23	-4,295	-936	-1,609	23,865	19,521	20,811	21,367
Monetary Movements	-5,177	15,200	12,318	44,767	29,545	28,982	33,286	7,234
Foreign Reserves	-1,234	1,817	-197	-15,729	-39,240	-16,183	12,767	7,482
Others	-3,943	17,017	12,515	60,496	68,785	45,165	20,519	-608
Errors & omissions	2,055	3,743	3,991	2,458	3,893	2,796	-22,008	-20,938

Source: Bank of Japan

As Table 2 shows, the current account surplus is presently being more than offset by Japanese direct and portfolio investments. Much of the intermediary function in the purchases of foreign stocks and bonds is naturally carried out by the London and New York outlets of the Japanese brokers, allowing them rapidly to expand their product lines and staff.

Internationalisation of the Yen

Another wave, greatly in favour of Japanese houses, is the internationalisation of their own currency. Until recently, the Japanese yen was hardly an international currency. It was not used much in trade invoicing, nor held in international reserves, nor borrowed in large amounts except in the form of Samurai bonds. That instrument — domestic yen bonds issued by foreign governments — was chiefly allowed by the Japanese government to offset balance of payments inflows and did not represent free access to Japanese liquidity.

The yen is now much more widely used internationally, owing to a variety of endogenous and exogenous forces, especially foreign political pressure. Euro-yen bonds for private sector companies were permitted in December 1984, followed by a succession of variants tapping longer-term Euro-yen sources. Obviously, Japanese houses had the best chance to dominate this market. Other aspects of internationalisation — the use of yen in trade and in the composition of international reserves, providing private placements in yen, and the listing of foreign shares in the Tokyo Stock Market — bring increased business opportunities to such Japanese sluices of liquidity.

3. The Ebb Tide

The Japanese banks, however, are now retrenching, and rather quickly. This can be seen both in statistical data and from anecdotal evidence. For example, the percentage of Japanese bank assets in the UK, as compared to the total assets of all banks here, has slipped from just over 30% in 1989 to 20% in January 1991. The Japanese share in international lending has fallen as well. From reports of City participants, one hears repeatedly that Japanese banks are not taking up their expected portions of syndicated loans, thus helping to drive up spreads. One hears as well of cancellation of Japanese lines of credit to European corporate borrowers, a segment they had formerly stressed.

Why has this reversal in strategy happened? Japanese trade surpluses are down, but are still large; the 1991 surplus should be around the level of 1990, and 1992 could even show an increase. The net deficit on the Japanese balance of payments may be a cause of yen weakness, but does not threaten the role of the Japanese financial houses. To the extent that Japanese investors continue to buy our stocks and bonds, and our companies, or invest in green field sites, this is still to the great benefit of the Japanese intermediaries. The massive losses on LDC debt of course hurt Japanese banks, but not nearly as much as American institutions. Firstly, they were not — as a group — as heavily involved in LDC debt, especially to Latin America, as were US banks. Secondly, those loans were mostly booked in US dollars. The appreciation of the yen over the 1980s has virtually halved the resultant writeoffs.

a) Temporary Concerns

There are a host of immediate explanations.

■ The Japanese banks, like all of us, are subject to BIS capital requirements, an area fully explored by other speakers at this Summer School. They have to meet the well-known 8% capital adequacy requirements next year. In a macho spirit, the Japanese banking fraternity indicated that they would do so by March 1991. Of course, they were allowed to count unrealized gains on their stock market profits up to 40% of Tier II capitalization. In a rising market, this gave Japanese banks a huge, and much commented on, advantage. But when the Tokyo stock market crashed by some 45% in 1990, their resultant capital calculation was decimated: by 31 March 1991, only two of the major banks in Japan could meet their self-inflicted goal. Thus they have attempted to control asset growth sharply, causing lack of commitment to new Euro loans and even to bilateral facilities.

■ This restrictive force is abetted by the tight monetary policy of the Bank of Japan. Since mid-1989, the Bank of Japan has hiked local interest rates five times in an attempt to cut what was by Japanese standards an alarming rate of inflation. It also instituted a sharp credit control, in traditional fashion. Japanese banks were, and still are in early 1991, subject to direct credit expansion ceilings.

■ The collapse of the Stock Market paralleled fears of a similar collapse of a similarly inflated real estate market. Speculation in Japan had been rife in the late 1980s, resulting in the famous "bubbles" in the equity and land markets. If the property market crashes — it is down a bit, but not as far as Bank of Japan's Governor Mieno would accept — the banks' assets, especially their massive loans to property investors, would deteriorate. Some of this is already in evidence — the Itoman scandal involving Sumitomo Bank for instance — and much damage could still come.

■ Compounding these worries, corporate bankruptcies in Japan in general have accelerated. From a decade-low of Y1.2 trillion in 1989, 1990's total corporate bankruptcies amounted to Y2 trillion. More alarmingly, January 1991 brought Y400 billion of bankruptcies in a single month. According to *The Economist* of 27 April 1991, Japanese sources predict these to rise to Y4 trillion in 1993. If BIS ratios are under water, loans to property speculators highly suspect, regular corporate loans themselves weakening, profits down, then already dubious international lending will itself be held back.

■ International lending continues in the doldrums. The volume of new deals has shrunk. Some spreads have risen, but many observers would conclude that today's margins for good borrowers still do not give us bankers a decent return on equity. Lending to British building societies at 25 bp or to Italian savings institutions at 37.5 bp, even if 0.2 weighted for capital adequacy calculations, does not quite pay the piper.

■ Foreign portfolio investment is also sharply down. Owing to tight money in Japan, higher interest rates have wiped out the prevailing interest rate differential between the yen and especially the dollar, diminishing the appetite of Japanese investors for foreign securities.

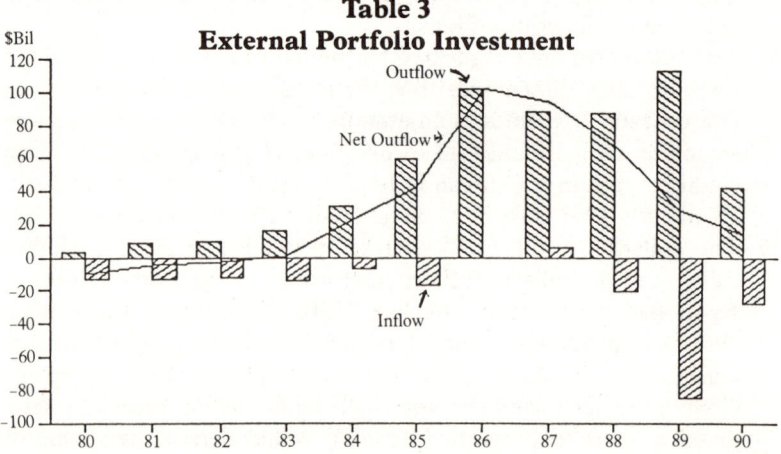

Table 3
External Portfolio Investment

b) More Long-Lasting Concerns

The above problems are probably temporary ripples and may disappear. Broader, structural concerns are shifting Japanese bank strategies, too.

Changes in Article 65

Real liberalization of the Tokyo markets is but a matter of time. The artificial barriers between banking and broking are bound to be reduced sharply. In a typical Japanese compromise, the most likely structure is for banks to have a separate underwriting subsidiary and for the securities houses to have subsidiaries allowed to undertake certain types of wholesale banking. This will not emulate the German/Swiss model of universal banking, strongly opposed by the big brokers, nor the evolving fashion of *Allfinanz*, but should create a system allowing more transparency of operations and more control, if legal and possible anti-trust problems are sorted out. "Firewalls" to avoid conflicts of interest are much discussed. But shortly (1993/1994?) the big four securities houses could possess bank subsidiaries which would transact foreign exchange, issue CDs, and lend to wholesale customers. Commercial banks could have an investment banking arm able to underwrite securities in the primary market and sell them throughout their branch networks. Intense competition can be expected, also more attention to home matters, now that most Japanese banks have established their external base.

Tokyo as a True Financial Centre

As a result of domestic liberalization and all the trends already mentioned, Tokyo will increasingly play a role as a true world financial centre. Even with the internationalization of the yen, access to yen liquidity and continuing economic strength, Tokyo is not — yet — a market of the depth and breadth of London or New York. A smaller number of international players is represented and some of these compete only in limited areas. New product innovation is minimal. Regulation and restrictive tax practices linger on. Yet Tokyo is inexorably moving towards true status as a world centre, different from London's turntable market because it represents the big aqueduct of domestic liquidity. Its financial houses want to be fully competitive there as well as abroad.

135

A good example of competition at home is in the securities sector. Tokyo has not had a "Big Bang", nor is it likely to, but there has been a steady reduction of brokerage commissions and a steady influx of foreign stockbrokers (after great pressure from the UK and US governments). Foreign brokers, against all expectations, have captured a material share of the Japanese securities market, nearly as big as that of the Big Four. Anyone who would have predicted this five years ago would have been ridiculed, partly because of the experience of foreign banks in Japan. As an example of the great success of the author in the latter area, I could relate the following: I was general manager of Morgan Guaranty in Tokyo for four years from 1976 to 1980. In 1976, the six dozen foreign banks in Japan had 3% of total banking assets in the country. When I left in 1980, we collectively had 2%.

This percentage is not much bigger now: foreign banks which have not closed their operations in Tokyo typically use them as support for the more lucrative area of securities transactions and provision of related foreign exchange and derivative products.

There is even in banking, however, a worrying attack on another Japanese bank prerogative: their guarantees of foreign bond issues of Japanese corporates. Owing to the previous very high credit rating of the Japanese banks, and relative unfamiliarity about most Japanese corporations, the Japanese banks guaranteed many foreign bonds, allowing the corporate issuer lower costs. Now the main rating agencies have begun to downgrade Japanese bank ratings; there are no Triple A rated Japanese commercial banks anymore. (Norinchukin, the giant agricultural co-operative bank, and Nomura Securities maintain AAA ratings.) Further downgradings are possible. Thus Japanese corporate bonds in European markets are likely to have European banks as their guarantors.

The fact that the strong securities markets in Japan is clearly penetrable by foreign players with excellent research and derivative products will much occupy the minds of Japanese bankers and brokers. The misery in Wall Street — due to its own excesses and greed — and the failures of almost anyone who bought a broker or jobber in the Big Bang period in London, will also diminish their appetite to grow abroad, and especially to make any large scale acquisitions. The disastrous results at Guinness Mahon, taken over by Bank of Yokohama in 1989, may increase their reluctance.

4. An Attempt at a Conclusion

I have tried in this paper to illustrate forces and flows which have pushed the Japanese banks into our markets and which may also sweep them back to Tokyo. I have used throughout the image of financial flows as water. And as water finds its own level, so do financial markets. Sam Goldwyn once said "Never predict anything, especially about the future". But I will try to make some guesses about forthcoming currents in Japanese banking and how its pumps (the banks) and dams (the regulators) will react.

Any abnormal financial currents eventually flow towards equilibrium. The huge Japanese trade surpluses will eventually shrink, as did the US ones (long ago) and the Arab surpluses more recently. Either the continued revaluation of the yen, the competition from the "Four Dragons" of South East Asia, trade barriers or increased domestic consumption — or more likely, some combination of all of these — will drive the surpluses down. Indeed, domestic spending, whether on better quality of life for the average Japanese or better national infrastructure, seems to me to be highly attractive and desirable for all parties. With lower incoming surpluses, the external capital flows will themselves slow somewhat.

If so, the conduits of these flows — the Japanese banks — will be less evident in our markets, and will need to build up their Western bases, if at all, at a lower rate.

And the forthcoming changes in Tokyo itself will focus Japanese banks' attention more sharply on matters at home. Why bother to build a very costly London underwriting base, in an over-supplied market, and miss out on opportunities in Japan? Most large Japanese houses, except some of the regional banks, have virtually completed their overseas structure. A global foundation, allowing 24 hour trading and including competent local staff, can be boasted by any of the city, trust and long-term banks and the securities houses. It may well be seen as high time to make sure the home base is still competitive and able to take advantage of the new Tokyo ballgame. The Japanese authorities will certainly want to ensure this as well.

So I think we may have seen the apogee of Japanese banks in our markets. What this means for direct competition with Western banks is not totally clear. The Japanese will still be very strong competitors at home and from home. They have established bases abroad which emulate those created earlier by the British, then the Americans, then

137

the Continentals. But outside Japan, they face the same high costs as do Western banks and the same overcapacity in banking. There is no hidden Japanese advantage — in cost, customer base or innovation — which makes Japanese banks more competitive than any other national group. Indeed, interest rate deregulation in Japan is going to hurt their profitability for some time. Their advantage has always been the strong cohesion of Japanese industry with its banks, and above all, the role they play as intermediaries in the river of Japanese external flows. As that river slows down, so must inevitably the rapid expansion of the Japanese banking industry abroad.

Reading List for Japanese Finance

T Adams and I Hoshii *A Financial History of the New Japan*, Tokyo: Kodansha, 1972.

Daniel Burstein *Yen! Japan's New Financial Empire and its Threat to America*, New York: Simon and Schuster, 1988.

Bill Emmott* *The Sun Also Sets: Why Japan will not be Number One*, London: Simon and Schuster, 1989.

Bill Emmott** 'The Ebb Tide', Supplement to *The Economist*, 27 April 1991.

Chalmers Johnson *MITI and the Japanese Miracle*, Tokyo: Charles Tuttle, 1986.

Andreas R Prindl *Japanese Finance*, Chichester: Wiley, 1981.

Andreas R Prindl 'Money in the Far East', Supplement to *Banking World*, Summer 1986.

Yoshio Suzuki *Money and Banking in Contemporary Japan*, New Haven: Yale University Press, 1980.

Yoshio Suzuki *The Japanese Financial System*, Oxford: Oxford University Press, 1988.

Karel van Wolferen *The Enigma of Japanese Power*, New York: Macmillan, 1989.

For those with limited reading time available, I recommend these, both by Bill Emmott:

*This is the revisionist theory: that Japan has only a short-lived window of opportunity, and riches, before financial, political and demographic forces shut the window. While it is not solely on finance or banking, the present financial flows permeate the book.

**The most recent *Economist* supplement on International Finance.

Developing Strategy to 2000

Lord Alexander of Weedon, QC, FCIB
*Chairman, National
Westminster Bank*

Lord Alexander of Weedon, QC, FCIB

Born in 1936, Robert Alexander is a Cambridge graduate in English and law. He was called to the Bar in 1961 and made a Queen's Counsel in 1973. Since 1983 he has also been a QC in New South Wales. He was chairman of the Bar Council from 1985-86.

In 1987 he was appointed chairman of the Panel on Takeovers and Mergers, a position he relinquished in 1989. He was created a life peer in 1988.

He became chairman of National Westminster Bank in October 1989, having joined the NatWest Board in May 1989 as a deputy chairman. A non-executive director of RTZ Corporation since January 1991, Lord Alexander has been a trustee of the National Gallery since 1986 and is also a trustee of *The Economist*. He is chairman of the Council of Justice, and of CRISIS — the charity for the homeless — and president of the Parkinson's Disease Society.

Contents

1. Introduction

There are two significant factors which should be borne in mind when discussing strategy. First of all, strategy tends to be evolutionary. It is not a series of "road to Damascus" conversions. Secondly, strategies must be developed and executed within the dynamics of the general economic environment. Thus any prediction of strategy, just as any prediction of the economic environment in the year 2000, is likely to be fragile, since it lacks the priceless benefit of hindsight and we all lack the ability to control external events.

However, if we are to undertake such prognostication, it is important that it be based on our experiences of the last decade. As Santayana put it, "Those who do not learn from the past are condemned to repeat it". By examining the principal influences of the past decade, we may find pointers to what the likely constraints are for banking in the next decade.

1980s Review

The banking industry during the 1980s underwent a process of substantial change. In the vanguard came deregulation, with the liberalisation of the building societies and the TSB in the UK. The former tacit acceptance of stable market shares has been severely challenged. Today, in the United Kingdom, all domestic financial services and markets are fully competitive in whatever kind of business a customer chooses to participate. Competition among the banks, both domestic and foreign, or with building societies and other near banks, has been particularly fierce. This benefits customers because it prevents excessive pricing in relation to the nature and risk of the business undertaken, and it sustains a keen pressure for quality of service.

However, there have been other consequences of change. With deregulation and the removal of exchange controls, we saw excessive liquidity in the market. This fuelled competition as too much money chased too little good business. The globalisation of the banking market created substantial integration of the wholesale markets and a common pricing. But the pricing margins became eroded to an unprofitable extent, with sometimes a consequential fall in lending standards to attract market share. Cheaper and cheaper credit was offered in both the personal mortgage and corporate sectors as the risk/reward ratio of the banks became unhinged.

Both the deregulation of the financial services industry, and the perceived need to diversify income streams, led banks into markets in which they had little or no experience. They believed that knowledge and experience could be purchased alongside goodwill. The strong growth in the banks' balance sheets during the 1980s led banks to aspire towards global banking.

Deregulation, excessive liquidity, disintermediation and intensified competition in traditional markets, diversification into non-traditional markets, and finer pricing to win new business were not a healthy combination. As the US and UK economies went into recession, and the impending capital adequacy requirements imposed by the Basle Committee began to be felt, a dramatic decline in 1990 in reported earnings and increase in domestic debt provisions by US and UK banks led to doubts as to whether a global credit crunch was imminent. With the tightening fiscal and monetary policies in Germany and Japan, and a slowing economic performance in Europe generally, the problems may no longer be so localised to Anglo-Saxon economies.

1990s?

In the UK, such boom and bust cycles have become almost ingrained in our economic culture. It is increasingly recognised that these cycles are inherently unhealthy. It is the degree of commitment to act on this realisation which is critical to all our progress. The importance of more stable, reliable growth cannot be overstated. We can only achieve this through the preservation of monetary stability and continuing low inflation. Industrial recovery is a prerequisite of a stronger financial sector. A bank's customer base, its staff and its investors are all dependent upon such stable growth.

Shareholders expect banks to operate as businesses, rather than as institutions. So there is an increasing need for customers to recognise that their banks can no longer be regarded as public utilities offering a multitude of services at subsidised prices. The obvious corollary is that if customers have to pay more, they will be less inclined to tolerate inefficiencies and there will be a continuing focus on the quality of service provided.

Banks will also continue to develop the technological systems to drive down the heavy cost burden imposed by their vast branch networks, the cost of money transmission and high staffing levels. So remote banking will develop further and must be fashioned to meet customer demand. Yet the pace of such change must match the pace at which people increasingly feel comfortable with such facilities. These developments will obviously impact on the banks' branch structures. As a generalisation, the result will be a drastic slimming down of these structures.

Banks will have to be increasingly specialised in the services they offer, only diversifying into those activities which provide adequate financial reward. The pressures on balance sheet growth imposed by minimum capital adequacy requirements will be a constraint, a discipline and an influence on strategy.

With capital continuing to restrict balance sheet growth, banks will need to look for new ways to meet shareholders' demands and support capital growth through retentions. They will seek to diversify into selective markets which offer high fee-earning potentials.

Both in the manner of their diversification and in the different levels of capital strengths, banks will become less and less similar to each other over the next decade. Moreover, the pressure on banks not to waste valuable capital resources through provisioning, and the need for careful management of diversification, will mean that risk controls and systems will become more sophisticated. This can only be salutary.

The one prophetic certainty is that banking in the year 2000, provided that it continues to offer a service of quality, will remain of immense importance to society. Our industry does not always escape criticism — from governments, shareholders and consumer groups — but it remains a central dynamo of the economy. The transmission of money may seem a prosaic activity to which people give relatively little thought, but it is vast in size and scope. For example, NatWest's automated teller machines carry out 160 million transactions a year. Our Stone Data Centre processes some four million transactions a day. Banks will continue to develop and modernise their technology to provide cheaper and more efficient processing, and truncation may be prominent, but in one way or another transmission of funds will be central. Similarly, traditional lending activities will always be required, whether to help new businesses start up, or existing businesses expand, whether to assist individuals in buying their homes or otherwise meeting customer needs. Banks must continue to provide responsible lending. This means providing the right financial instruments to satisfy the customer's needs and doing the best to make certain that he or she has the ability to meet his or her financial responsibilities. We cannot vaunt our place in the community unless we meet people's true needs

147

in a thoroughly responsible way. The badge of a bank will need to be the badge of quality, dedication and skill.

This approach will marry with the spirit of a decade where fundamental virtues will reassume their importance. Society will place ever-increasing emphasis on education and training, investment in infrastructure and technology, and a greater awareness of the social and ecological environment in which we exist. This will provide the foundation upon which to increase our productivity and improve our competitive position within Europe. Banks are nothing if they do not at all times seek to promote sound development of the economy on which they depend for prosperity.

To summarise, the next decade *may* see:

- more stable economic growth and sustainable low inflation;
- banks continuing to be an essential dynamo of the economy through money transmission and traditional banking activities;
- banks' balance sheet growth restricted by continuing capital constraints;
- banks seeking less balance sheet-intensive business and looking to enhance fee-earning capacity;
- increasingly sophisticated risk control and portfolio management;
- banks being forced to be more selective in their diversification;
- banks focusing more on driving out inefficiencies;
- investors seeking more rewarding returns;
- banks providing a service of quality in order to justify higher charges to customers;
- the provision of a caring and helpful service to customers;
- society requiring banks to be responsible, primarily in their lending; but
- such social responsibility also extending to the provision of training, which will ensure that staff have the opportunity to meet their potential;
- a sophisticated community relations programme;
- the application of best practice on environmental standards both within the organisation and in lending policies; and
- encouragement of savings to underpin the need for infrastructure investment.

All aspects of banking will have to be executed within the context of its customers' needs within the wider European market.

If the decade *does* see these developments, then we shall be able to approach the millenium in good order.

2. Banking as a Business

Sheltered Markets

This may seem an unnecessary starting-point. Is not all commercial activity a business? In the case of banks, there has in the past been a somewhat ambivalent approach. Until the last decade, banks were in some countries regarded largely as institutions rather akin to public utilities. Most markets were regulated and indeed many markets were cartelised or oligopolised. The banks expected to receive adequate profits over the business cycle. In the United States, this was caricatured as 3-6-3 banking, meaning that you took deposits at 3 per cent, lent at 6 per cent, and went home at 3 pm to play golf.

In the United Kingdom, the banks were similar in structure and were protected from domestic competition by legislation. The trustee savings banks and the building societies were prevented from operating in the main banking markets. Competition was limited, and the incentives to improve service not over-intense. The organic growth of the market largely satisfied the more aggressive banks' aspirations for expansion.

There were benefits from this structure — many of them for bankers, but some for society. The banks were stable, with relatively similar performances. Regulation was conducted as much implicitly or by "governor's eyebrows" as explicitly. Banks could be relied upon to help out when difficulties arose with individual rescues or lifeboats. The service offered to the industrial and commercial sector came under some criticism, but was generally adequate for its time. The social and economic roles of banks and of bankers were well established and indeed useful. It was also convenient for the regulator.

Competitive Markets

That world now seems somewhat quaint, which indicates the vast changes which have occurred in less than a decade. There has been the worldwide deregulation of the commercial marketplace. Almost all protection of market positions has been removed. In the United Kingdom, the government has deliberately adopted a policy of commercial deregulation, liberalising the trustee savings banks and the building societies and increasing competition at all levels. With "Big Bang", the divide between brokers and jobbers was also removed, allowing banks to own market makers and freeing up commissions.

In Europe we are seeing the effects of the Second Banking Directive in establishing an open marketplace for banking across the Community, to be followed in due course by an Investment Service Directive doing the same thing for capital markets' business and investment advice.

Exchange controls have either already been or soon will be abolished in most OECD countries. Under pressure from the United States and Europe, Japan has begun to liberalise its marketplace. This has generated intense competitive pressure in the wholesale markets, as it did in the UK when we abolished our controls in 1979, and we have seen technological developments which have enabled customers to arbitrage between products in almost any marketplace and any currency, although the worldwide spread of information through technology means that pricing anomalies are removed extremely quickly. Aggressive entrants into the business, allying their entrepreneurship with modern technology, have created new products which could challenge the old ones in terms of both price and quality. Securitisation and disintermediation have put intense price competition on to the banks.

Customers are better informed, and thereby more sophisticated and discerning. Newspapers have weekly features telling customers where to find the best borrowing and deposit rates. Once an established oligopolised or cartelised market is challenged then it becomes virtually impossible to put it back together again. It seems certain that the markets will remain open and competitive.

Bank Shares

The banks are also being treated by the stock market like any other business. The balance sheet liabilities of a bank represent money and, as such, are likely to grow in line with the money supply. Given steady economies in the use of money, or increases in the velocity of circulation, the money supply is unlikely over a long period to grow sharply in real terms.

On the asset side of the balance sheet, there will clearly be a limit to the amount of business a bank can support in relation to its capital and, by extension, the amount of business supportable by the banking system as a whole. As a result of the Basle Agreement, such capital is bound to grow in a more measured way, through retained earnings and capital raising. Under these circumstances, it is unlikely that in the foreseeable future the banking system will again be able to support the surge in lending which took place during the 1980s.

So, through their traditional business, the growth of balance sheet banking is likely to be modest in real terms over the next decade, and this creates an inevitable impetus to seek new income streams. Bank shares will, as in the past, continue to be more valued for dividend than for capital growth.

Improving return on equity in order to build capital, satisfy investor requirements, and provide protection against a hostile acquisition, will force banks to look for increasing earnings growth. Whether by writing fee-earning securities business, or providing insurance business, or offering processing services, many banks will become financial service conglomerates. The pressure for earnings growth can be a major driving factor in relation to the strategy of banks and as regards their business and risk philosophies. However, in contrast to the 1980s, banks' diversification will be much more focused and more selective, with more rigorous returns criteria being applied. The drive now is much more for profitability and return on equity, rather than for simple headline profits and balance sheet size. To be a financial service conglomerate does not involve seeking to be a "global" bank.

3. Banks as Risk-Bearing Institutions

The pressure on banks to perform as businesses raises the question of whether banks are in fact the same as, or are markedly different from, other companies.

What distinguishes banking from other businesses is that its raw material is deposits, which are then risked in a controlled manner so as to obtain profit. If trust between a bank and its depositors is ever broken, then the business quickly founders.

One obvious feature of banks is that they bear considerable risks. Their income stream is largely from margins on loans, which might imply that banks should always go for low risks. A venture capital company will obtain a large profit on its successful investments, so can afford to make a significant proportion of failed investments. But a bank, with its lending margin measured as a few percentage points, or even a few basis points, has to aim for every loan being successful.

Banks face other major areas of risk. One relates to the payments system, which in many countries is managed by the banks. The banks' exposure to default in such systems may be colossal. About £90 billion a day is cleared through the UK CHAPS system, and about $4,000 billion each day through the Federal Reserve Bank of New York. The fees earned on this business are relatively small in relation to each transaction. The cost to the banks and society if the system broke down could be catastrophic. A highly risk-averse posture is thus appropriate for commercial banks as regards two major areas of risk: lending and transmission. The up-side is limited, since the return is a narrow margin or small fee, while the down-side is enormous since there is virtually no limit to the potential losses as a consequence of poor controls. This has led to a risk-averse culture within banks.

The issue which arises is how an institution, based quite rightly upon a risk-averse culture, will develop when it is faced with the normal run of commercial pressures which affect the majority of companies. The commercial pressure is to obtain greater earnings. This problem was compounded during the 1980s, when there was such excess capital in banking, stemming largely from the massive expansion of Japanese banks. As a consequence, the returns on normal banking business were driven down to extremely low levels.

In attempting to obtain the normal remuneration, and maintain market shares, the temptation for banks is, perhaps inadvertently, to lower their risk standard in their mainstream business. The risk/reward ratio becomes unhinged when the probability of loan loss is considerably greater than would be appropriate for the margins being achieved. Lending-led expansion is always dangerous for banks because of the risk that it allows.

Other dangers may arise if banks go into new businesses. Some businesses may be unprofitable simply because that market is already oversupplied. In other cases, the banks may take on excessive risk through lack of risk appreciation or risk control. In other areas, and distributing insurance is one, the banks have been able to obtain extra income relatively safely. Diversifying into businesses which are counter-cyclical to commercial banking will protect the overall stability of its earnings. What we are likely to see under such new conditions is much greater volatility in earnings, and a greater variation between the earnings levels of different banks as they diversify into different markets and adopt different strategies. At the end of the day, banks have to reconcile their commercial ambitions with the reality of the marketplace, but they must never forget that they have a unique risk structure. It is dangerous to ignore this.

These circumstances will increase the need for excellent risk management whilst making it more difficult to achieve. Equally, the very existence of risk emphasises the importance of central banks as lenders of last resort. They are not there to encourage or protect inefficiency, but to fulfil a vital role in the preservation of confidence of depositors in the reliability of the system. The regulatory role of supervisors, whether or not they are central banks, serves the same purpose.

What will be required to meet these challenges?

Decentralisation of business decisions alongside greater diversity, and complexity, or risk, will need:

- reliance on competent, well-trained and flexible management;
- good information systems;
- strong independent control and audit systems; and
- clear and consistent corporate leadership, which creates an environment in which risk and reward are appropriately balanced, and decision-makers do not feel pressured to be either too risk averse, or to pursue income or market share beyond the point justified by the reward in that particular business.

The banks' strategic planners will have to think carefully about the balance of high risk/high reward, and low risk/low return businesses. They will also need to focus on the degree to which they can identify business areas which are counter-cyclical, or which are relatively stable performers, to offset more volatile sectors or jettison mature businesses which are no longer capable of producing adequate returns.

Corporate structure will also be important. Banks as financial institutions will increasingly operate in a variety of businesses with differing risk/reward characteristics and with quite distinct types of employees. Individual businesses will need to have considerable responsibility for their own operations, which must include the management of risk, but there will need to be a degree of corporate oversight and control.

The creation and integration of a corporate structure which balances these conflicting pressures properly will be crucial to proper risk management given the need in a large, diverse, decentralised group to rely on management training, information systems and effective independent checks.

There is a further issue linked to risk which is the role of the regulators. We have seen in recent years substantial commercial deregulation in banking. Access to markets has been made easier. Virtually no markets are sheltered now. At the same time supervisors have become yet more conscious of their responsibilities. We have seen further international co-operation between regulators and we have seen new methods of regulation being introduced. These have in many ways been more legalistic than the previous systems, because they had to operate explicitly, rather than privately and informally. One of the main elements of the new system is the collection of far more information by central banks and supervisors and the much closer monitoring of the position which the banks may take in credit and securities markets. In addition, control ratios have been applied, most notably the BIS capital adequacy standards. This may lead to the paradox that reconciling a regulated risk-bearing business with the commercial marketplace is insoluble. An example of such paradox is the need to balance profit retentions to support capital growth and meet BIS standards, whilst meeting shareholder expectations with adequate dividend payout.

The natural reaction of regulators is that, if they see an industry or company which is weak, they will seek tighter standards. This can, however, be counterproductive if such regulation stifles any chance of recovery. We are seeing at the moment in the US the tightrope which regulators are walking between cautious regulation, which encourages investor confidence, and over-regulation, the cost of which can be the final straw to break a bank.

4. Capital

Balance Sheet Constraints

The most recent regulatory controls on banking, the adoption of the Basle capital ratios, will have a profound effect upon banking and indeed upon the banks' relationship with the rest of the financial and economic systems. The Basle ratios create a mechanical linkage between the capital a bank has and its weighted risk assets. The total capital in the banking system will be constrained, and can grow only moderately. One source of equity capital is retained earnings. This should be positive, and should increase bank capital in real terms.

Nevertheless, banking is a competitive business. Rates of return may be in the attractive commercial range, but the industry as a whole will not obtain extraordinary returns. This puts a natural constraint on the total increase in retained capital.

A second source of equity will be rights and other capital issues. These can be made when the market is accessible. We must bear in mind that the market requires a certain return before it will invest capital in a business. Unless there is earnings potential in the business, capital will not be available. Thus, any financial constraints that exist in relation to potential earnings per share and return on capital will limit the extent to which any bank, and therefore the banking system as a whole, may attract investment through equity issues.

Tier 2 capital, such as subordinated debt, is relatively cheap, and may be obtained on the back of a bank's equity capital. Nevertheless, at times those markets, too, may be either closed or much more expensive than at other times. Tier 2 capital cannot be taken for granted at all times.

As far as an individual bank is concerned, it is not possible to do more business in weighted risk asset terms than is allowed by the capital ratios. So banks with good earnings and good capital growth will expand, whereas those with declining capital will have to contract their assets. The increasingly transparent tiering between well- and less well-capitalised banks will be exacerbated by tighter regulation and the inability of those weaker banks to access the equity markets.

Apart from the microeconomic effects on individual banks, this ratio system applies to banks as a whole. The total weighted risk assets of the entire banking system can be no greater than that allowed by the total capital of the banking system. This means that once the banks are fully lent, or once the banks reach a situation where their total weighted risk assets are in line with their total capital, then from that point on the growth of weighted risk assets is dependent upon the capital growth achieved.

Liquidity or Credit Crunch?

The rapid growth in lending which took place worldwide during the 1980s is unlikely to happen again for the foreseeable future. We need to ask ourselves whether such a constraint matters. What should be the true long-term growth of bank assets and therefore the business it can write?

Another variant of this is to ask whether it matters if banks can lend less quickly than companies require to borrow in a boom. The availability of banks' capital is unlikely to enable them to accommodate significant economic cycles, even if the underlying trend may be acceptable. The likely development of this pressure over the years is that banks will first do their transactions with the most profitable business areas, which tends to mean the retail customers and small- and medium-sized companies. There could thus be a steady squeeze on the general availability of credit to the largest companies.

How much excess liquidity is there in the corporate sector? How much can companies afford to pay for their credit? What clearly will happen is that the price of credit to this sector will increase, as indeed it has done. If the industry reaches a point where the pricing of credit to all sectors, including to the big companies, covers the cost of capital, then we shall meet the precondition for capital investment to re-enter into the industry on a relatively large scale. In this way the capacity of the banking industry and the potential demand for loans will reach equilibrium, albeit imperfectly and, as Adam Smith recognised, only for a time.

A credit crunch could be defined as a time when banks are unreasonably unwilling to lend, or when the capacity of the banking system is no match for what is required. We have not reached that point. Indeed, there is at the moment no reason to believe that banks are refusing credit unreasonably in any country. The question of the relationship between the capacity to lend and worldwide demand will be under discussion, but there are at present no such problems, although there is probably now a wider divergence of interest margins than a decade or so ago, reflecting a more careful assessment of risk.

Capital Ratios Driving Pricing

What the Basle ratios are doing in a significant way is *driving* pricing policy. Banks can now work out precisely the capital cost of any element of their business. They cannot even afford to cross-subsidise between businesses, since all markets are competitive.

Securitisation of business increased dramatically during the 1980s and took some good business away from the banks. A significant part of this business was in fact backed by bank commitments, and thus was still a capital cost on the banking system. In as far as capital becomes tighter, then so some of these markets are in turn becoming

156

less liquid and pricing is beginning to reflect that fact. Indeed many companies which are perceived to be of poorer quality have found the US commercial paper market closed to them entirely, forcing them to rely more on the banking market. Nevertheless, as banks become more selective in the allocation of their assets, we may see faster disintermediation at the quality end of the corporate market as such companies use the securitised markets to a greater extent.

But a second impact may well be that banks will look more closely at securitising their own assets and selling them off to genuine investors such as pension funds, insurance companies and the corporate sector in order to create balance sheet capacity. We have seen in the United States substantial securitisation of credit card assets, consumer loans and some areas of corporate finance. Perhaps those business areas may move more to the UK and to the Continent.

5. Social Pressures

Caring and Commercial?

Although banks face increasing commercial pressures and will do so for the rest of this century, they will have to adapt their commercialism to the social pressures of the time. Although the markets see banks as companies, and they have to behave accordingly, the public, and particularly their customers, in many instances continue to view them as institutions. This creates an interesting dilemma. Banks are conspicuous; they are easy targets. Bankers traditionally have been regarded as good citizens and have wished so to regard themselves. In what might be termed the institutional phase of banking, bankers accepted restraint upon their commercial activity and in any case were happy to accept that discipline in exchange for reputation and esteem.

Many banking transactions tend to be a matter of one very large organisation transacting with an individual person who has little influence or leverage in the conduct of that transaction, and this naturally creates unease and tension. However, consumer groups are now well organised, and Members of Parliament speak up for their constituents, as they should. Strong pressures are there.

The situation is now more uneasy as banks are forced by competitive pressure to be much more selective and rational in the conduct of their business. Earning money is not easy, and requires initiatives in the form of sophisticated marketing which, in the eyes of some, would appear increasingly aggressive. Banks will make mistakes, either through thoughtlessness or in pure error. People may be offered credit who cannot handle it. As banks are busier, more active, more selective, then so at times they are bound to irritate some customers. During the 1990s, perhaps the "caring" decade, individuals may wish to transact their business with institutions with which they feel greatest empathy, and which most closely reflect their own outlook. This may affect employment as well as marketing policy. Will banks need to change their public stance to allow for this?

In the field of our relations with the personal sector, banks in the UK have faced the Jack Report, which criticises banks on some fundamental issues. Greater transparency in bank charges, confidentiality of customer information, and protection of customers from possible negligence costs, are all highlighted as concerns by consumer groups. The banks are currently drafting a voluntary code of practice in liaison with such consumer bodies. If banks are unable to provide a voluntary code, then it is quite possible that the government will introduce legislation. The banks have already created an ombudsman, whose decision is binding upon them. This is healthy: it gives the customer the opportunity of independent resolution of disputes without the cost involved in going to court.

Community and the Environment

The high street banks all have significant community programmes in place. They are major donors to charities, but more particularly they have been trend-setters in developing relevant and imaginative social initiatives. Whether it be in promoting the arts, sport or giving help to the disadvantaged, the banks have played, and continue to play, an active role in our society.

The environment is another major area of concern to the banks. We are aiming to achieve environmental best practice throughout our business activities. For example, we are reviewing our lending practices and, at a "housekeeping" level, ensuring that all our company cars will run on lead-free petrol by the end of this year. Our new data centre at Stone is designed to use far less energy than that of other computer centres and is cheaper to run. We are more environmentally conscious because it makes social, business and commercial sense. The "polluter pays" principle will encourage others to follow our example as the law and standards tighten around them.

Banks may face heavy costs and loss of revenue if land held as their security is found to be contaminated and the lender forced to pay the historic costs of cleaning up. In the United States, the Comprehensive Environmental Response Compensation and Liability Act goes a long way to increasing the potential liability of banks and there have already been some very worrying cases. In the EC there are 280 legally binding environmental measures and further major legislation is likely in the short term, both at national and international levels.

These and other social issues will need to be managed very carefully over the next decade.

6. Europe

A Bigger Backyard

Some of the major developments of recent years have been in Europe. Our home market has increased from 56 million, the UK population, to the 340 million people in the EC. Other countries are already applying for membership or considering doing so. Similarly the legal and regulatory framework in which we operate is EC-wide and development of our strategies must take this into account. To date we at NatWest have few complaints.

Much has already happened, notably the Second Banking Directive. The 1992 process continues and it is certain that development will not cease on 1 January 1993.

The perception that the UK is increasingly taking its rightful place in the construction of Europe for the 21st century is to be warmly welcomed. The last 40 years have been littered with examples of the UK missing the opportunity to help shape the future of Europe, which has nevertheless taken form without our assistance or our interests being properly protected.

Here the current Inter-Governmental Conferences on Political and Economic and Monetary Union are crucial. For a financial services group, it is vital that the UK be fully on the inside of institution building in Europe. Britain has nothing to fear from the goal of ultimate monetary union in Europe and we support that goal. But the pace must be driven by commercial impetus and mutual economic benefit and not just by ideology.

Banking on Europe

Monetary integration in Europe will have a major effect upon all the

159

financial markets. One of the major impacts will be simply from the greater intensity of competition. Barriers to entry into markets will be further removed. The Basle ratios will make the provision of credit and its pricing extremely competitive. Banks will have to get used to open markets, together with stable low inflation and probably a much greater focus on fee income rather than on interest margins.

Currently, the transmission and settlement systems differ widely between European countries. In most cases they give a very efficient service, but they are relatively expensive and inefficient in making small payments between different countries, where the charges may be a significant proportion of the face value. The European Commission is very conscious of this point which has in the past frustrated so many of us in small transactions.

Transmission systems are a significant source of profit to banks. They also impose great investment costs and have, as we have discussed, inherent risks. The interaction between the existing interests and pressures from the politicians as regards future institutional change in Europe will also have a major impact upon the banking business and on the profitability of different services.

It is of considerable importance to banks how the activity of any new European Central Bank will be dispersed throughout the Community. So will the policy techniques to be be used by that bank to achieve its monetary objectives. When there is a single currency, government paper in that unit will be traded in most of the financial centres in Europe. Banks will have to adapt their trading functions to deal with that situation.

Similarly, it will be important to know how present close relationships between commercial banks and their central bank will be translated into new arrangements with any European Central Bank.

Outside of specific measures aimed at financial institutions, there are many likely developments which will affect banks in the EC, including the Social Action programme, corporate governance, the environment, data protection and the external relations of the EC with non-EC Europe, the rest of the developed world and less developed countries. We must strive to ensure that the EC does not become, in itself, a protectionist trading block.

Europe is not a separate issue. I regard it as fundamental and adding a further dimension to most of the other issues which will confront us over the next decade, presenting challenges to which the best and fittest institutions will rise.

7. Management

The development of the staffing of banks is a major and very complicated theme in relation to how banks will adapt themselves to a different future. We have examined the transition of banking over the past decade from being partly institutional to being essentially a business.

Before these changes, the major risk taken by banking was in the credit area. All banks put enormous emphasis on credit training, and the route to the top usually included a position in a lending control function.

The underlying business structure was stable, so there was no need for entrepreneurship. Banking was a business where mistakes could cost more money than innovation could gain. With limited technological change, there was emphasis on sound, reliable administration. This fitted with mainly school-leaver recruitment, which provided the junior and middle management with sufficient talent within that cadre to produce the top management as required. Specialist functions were relatively few, so the vast bulk of the staff were recruited on the same basis.

This situation had its faults, but many virtues. Loyalty was extremely high. People who had been in a bank 20 or 30 years knew it extremely well, so the grapevine worked exceptionally efficiently. There were many failsafe mechanisms which could deter the organisation from making unnecessary mistakes. Many of the young school leavers deserved further education, but did not get the chance. Banks gave them the opportunity to fulfil their potential. It was commercially very efficient for its time.

Conditions have now greatly changed. Banks need a far larger number of specialists, and these are likely to have a professional loyalty as well as an employer loyalty. The range now includes engineers and computer experts, advanced mathematicians, and a host of other specialists.

Their terms of engagement have clearly to take into account professional as well as organisational factors, reflecting their skills and potential. How long will these professionals expect to stay with one company?

The banks now have to take what might be termed purely commercial decisions. Those who are marketing credit cards or other products have to know how to deal with what is essentially a retail marketing situation. We need people with commercial skills which might be more recognised in the generality of commerce than in banking.

As people reach higher levels in a bank, traditional lending skills become extremely important. But people also have to be able to run a business in terms of cost ratios, monitoring investment programmes, and getting the right balance of price, quality and service which will attract the customer. These are what might be termed "businessman's skills".

At the highest level, running a bank, a large bank, implies the same strategic skills as running any major multinational corporation. The full gamut of investor relations, capital funding, handling the stock market, deployment of resources, generation of income streams and control of costs, are all everyday matters on the desks of our top executives.

The complexity of personnel management is enhanced by the far wider range of skills now needed. The banks have no difficulty in recruiting people of the appropriate intelligence and skills. They can be given experience. The question is how one mixes that into an appropriate career pattern which gives early responsibility and adequate remuneration, whilst providing the necessary experience.

Even, or especially, in this brave new world banks need loyal, capable, careful staff, and many skilled, potentially mobile workers feel a need for some stability and security. We cannot forget that banking is a risk business. Disloyal, carefree staff can do enormous damage to a bank, and no reliance on systems can completely remove that risk.

Banks need now to know at an earlier stage what people's limits are in relation to taking on commercial and business responsibility. Whether someone can judge a situation, how good he or she is in determining the commercial possibility of a situation, are matters which we now need to know much earlier.

This implies testing and advancing some people much earlier in their career. People have to be tested and given the opportunity of learning, which means the opportunity of making mistakes, in a controlled environment, much earlier than has been the case in the past. If we want potential captains of industry by the age of 50, then people have to be tested severely not long after they are 40, and stretched significantly not long after they are 30. The task of getting the right top management creates issues which impact right down through the organisation and throughout career development for the future.

Pay systems based on deferred gratification are likely to come under very strong pressure, as people see their environment as more risky and wish to see the rewards for their efforts sooner rather than later or even perhaps never.

The banks approach these problems from a cost base which is in many cases relatively high. Achieving the appropriate cost base in relation to the revenue from particular businesses is a continuing process, which is in itself difficult and sometimes painful, and may overlay all the other trends which are occurring. Maintaining the loyalty of core employees, whilst asking some to leave before they had hoped, is not an easy equation. I do not think we have failed badly at this so far, but I could hardly say that we have found a definitive answer. It also means that although modern challenges are exciting, they have a real element of pain.

The culture of banks will clearly change under these market pressures. The ultimate requirement of a commercial company is to survive in its marketplace. It must be profitable. The culture of a bank will change right from the boardroom to the messenger lobby. A trite example is that the managers' luncheon room is increasingly becoming a place for functional refreshment rather than providing a privilege of office.

That culture will be more business-like, less hierarchical, more challenging, less institutional, more uncertain and more meritocratic, with equal opportunities at all levels being essential. Creating such a culture poses perhaps the greatest challenge to a bank. If the staff have the feeling that the bank knows where it is going, then they will fit their behaviour within this overall pattern and morale will be high. But if individual uncertainty is combined with a corporate feeling of drift then the problems may become acute.

8. Conclusion

Over the coming decade the banks will face a testing time in a variety of fields. These include social policy, management development, adaptation to changing technology, product innovation, increasing competition, changing regulatory patterns, and the need to form a coherent strategy to deal with all these matters.

As bankers, we cannot ignore the importance of the creation of a single European market. At present there are major differences between banks in the different countries. The monetary policy techniques differ, thus changing the operational and business pressures on banks. Payment and settlement systems vary widely, creating different combinations of cost structures, income sources and risks. Cost levels vary widely. The rules on ownership and management of banks differ a great deal. The capital market valuation of banks varies. Investment controls still influence the way in which funds may be invested by long-term savings institutions. In practical terms, access to markets varies considerably.

When we have a single market, and more especially if and when we have a single currency, many of these differences will have been or will have to be removed. Adaptation to a common banking franchise and a common banking marketplace will not be the least of the challenges facing banks.

BankExec-International

Timothy D. Dondlinger

Tim Dondlinger is a management consultant specializing in computer systems design and installation, computer training and management skills programmes. He holds a Bachelors Degree in Accounting/Business Administration and an MBA, both from Marquette University, Milwaukee.

He is a member of Far Cliffs Consulting, a human resources consulting organisation, and has worked on its bank simulation activities for several years. In 1986, he joined the Wisconsin Bankers' Association General Banking School to implement the use of personal computers into the BankSim program and, since 1989, he has complete operational responsibility for the introduction of the PC version of BankExec.

In 1990, he was an instructor and operations manager for BankExec International at the International Banking Summer School in Boston.

Charles Hoffman

Charles Hoffman joined the American Bankers' Association in 1975 as an economist in the Economic and Policy Research Division. In March 1985, he became Director of Executive Education with responsibility for planning and co-ordinating educational programmes for mid-level and senior banking officers, management of the computer-based simulation models and for planning and developing educational products.

He graduated from the University of California with a PhD in Economics and, before joining the ABA, he worked for the Department of Finance, State of California.

Elizabeth Lesan

Beth Lesan is Schools and Simulation Manager in the Executive Education Division of the American Bankers' Association with responsibility for the development, administration, marketing and sales of their computer-based bank management simulation models. In addition, she is Academic Director for the real estate, agri-finance and human resources schools for mid-level banking officers.

She graduated from Duke University and, prior to joining the ABA, she was an Assistant Vice President at First Union National Bank.

James W. Schreier

Jim Schreier is a management consultant specializing in management development and professional skills programmes. He is founder and president of Far Cliffs Consulting and, in addition to a PhD in Education, he also holds an MBA and Bachelors Degree in Business (Marketing and Human Resources) from Marquette University, Milwaukee.

He has worked extensively with the American Bankers' Association, the American Institute of Banking and other banks and banking organisations, both as an instructor and on the installation of simulation programs. Since 1977, he has been Administrator of the BankSim management training program and is also a member of the ABA BankExec Task Force.

In 1990, he was the administrator of the BankExec International program at the International Banking Summer School in Boston.

For 20 hours during formal sessions of the 1991 International Banking Summer School, and during countless other conversations looking at charts, debating strategies over breakfasts, lunch, and dinners, participants will have managed a $742m bank through a stormy economy and high-spirited competition. During the simulated year and a half, six quarters of 1996 and 1997, bank management teams will have faced decisions involving their overall strategy and the specific decisions involving their loan, deposit, and investment portfolios.

BankExec-International is an educational tool that can be characterized as a dynamic, interactive, short-run strategy game. It is designed to afford participants, who have varying levels of banking knowledge and sophistication, the opportunity to experience "hands-on" decision-making under conditions of an uncertain macroeconomic environment and uncertain competitive response. It provides immediate, detailed feedback for subsequent decisions.

The broad objectives of the BankExec-International program are:

1. To develop an awareness of the **interdependencies of various bank functions.**
2. To develop an understanding of the role and importance of **objectives and strategy in bank management.**
3. To create an awareness and understanding of the **inter-relationship of a bank with its dynamic and complex environments.**

In the International Banking Summer School, these broad goals interact with the specific goals of the School to give participants the opportunity to see the effects of some of the broader banking issues being discussed by speakers. Furthermore, with each bank management team composed of individuals from different countries and backgrounds, the simulation provides the format for an interesting comparison of banking practices. Spirited debates are stimulated over banking practices and various bank management strategies. Some of these debates can be ended by the deadlines associated with turning decisions in on time. Others go on being resolved over meals, at sports competitions, and at the various national parties. During the simulation, 30 individual bank management teams compete in four different financial communities. They experience different competitive and economic environments, which result in tremendous interest whenever charts showing the latest quarterly results are posted.

Getting Started

Before the International Banking Summer School started, participants completed an assignment evaluating the starting financial position of the simulated institution. Participants quickly discovered that they were taking over the management of a struggling bank. The bank had been growing quickly with erratic earnings. During the first BankExec session, participants have to discuss the starting financial package and set a course for their bank by considering a mission statement — and responding to goals set by the bank's board of directors. Specific assignments, management style, and organizational structure quickly become important as the teams organize themselves for the simulation. In each group, two bank management teams are formed with the two individual banks considering part of a broader bank holding company. The individual banks do not compete against each other in the same community. Decisions made in the first couple of sessions usually set the pattern for the whole course — for better or worse. Individual teams set strategies, monitor competition, and respond to the changes in the economy and community marketplace.

The Group Leaders play a key role in the success of the International Banking Summer School. Their broad role as "hosts" for groups of 15-16 bankers, and their specific role as facilitators of the group discussions, is intensified in the BankExec experience. In addition to breaking the larger group up into two banks, the Group Leaders function as instructors for the BankExec process. The Group Leaders combine their own IBSS experience with their banking experience, with their training in the BankExec program, and with their experience working with a diverse group of individuals, to work closely with the BankExec management teams during the decision-making process.

Much of BankExec's success is attributable to its interactive approach to education. The simulation allows participants to put newly-gained information into action, to test theories, and to take financial and management risks, in order to learn more about bank management in today's dynamic environment. This interactive learning approach naturally creates a challenging role for the group leaders, who must maintain a constant balance as both catalysts and hands-off managers in the simulation process, acting as facilitators and mentors, but carefully avoiding "managing" the students and ultimately managing their banks. Group Leaders find it difficult at times to step back and let teams make less than ideal management decisions for their banks, but it is important that they allow participants to achieve the maximum learning experience by sometimes making mistakes and gaining invaluable lessons from their results.

Success Factors

At the first formal session for BankExec the BankExec Administrator provides an overview of the simulation process and a presentation explaining how participants can get the most out of this learning experience. He emphasises the experiential nature of the BankExec program, and discusses the "discovery learning model" upon which the program is based. Participants are told about the difficulty of the first decision period, how they will be taking over a bank, having been given a wealth of information, but in an environment where most of them will want more information — and will be unsure what to do with the information they already have.

The BankExec process is one in which there is confusion and uncertainty in the early decisions, followed by the feeling of not understanding what's happening — but not being sure why — followed by new confidence in the ability to understand and react to the information that's been generated. It's a process much like learning to ride a bicycle. No one has ever learned from viewing an instructional videotape. Everybody struggles at first — and probably falls down a few times. The BankExec banks experience the same struggles and falls as they move through their management tenure.

There is emphasis on the importance of dealing within the economic and regulatory environment created by the simulation. Participants from widely differing countries, economically, socially, and politically, have to work together to make decisions for their BankExec bank. Participants tend to respond with decisions based on their own banks' experiences and their own particular market and regulatory framework. In the early discussions about the BankExec bank, participants are heard saying, "this isn't my bank" or "this is exactly what my bank faced last year." The discussion of basic banking concepts, trends, and issues that follows enables the students to broaden their conceptual framework by focusing on alternative strategies used by other bankers worldwide, and is exactly the desired outcome of the simulation in the International Banking Summer School.

BankExec also provides a "well of learning", with something there for everybody. Some participants are fairly quiet during team decisions, observing the decision-making process and learning from the comments of others. Other participants actively take over the management of the bank and spend additional time analysing the results. Each participant takes as little — or as much — as he or she wants from the learning experience. The BankExec model is also sophisticated enough, with the support provided by the BankExec administration, to prevent any group from fatally wounding either the bank or its learning experience. Some banks do very well overall, others experience average performance, some banks struggle throughout. But they all leave with a glow of learning and fun.

The First Decision

The first decision, for many teams, is the most difficult. Because all banks start from the same competitive position — with a set of financial reports that are identical — there is little competitive information on what other banks in the community might do. Each bank is forced to chart its management course in a relative vacuum of community information. Once the first decision is processed, the teams get several reports showing how competing banks are pricing their products and services. And like the real world, they have information on the loan rates charged by all competing banks. But during the first decision, the teams wrestle with the unfamiliarity of the reports — and the need to speculate on what types of strategies other banks might implement.

Each simulated bank team must decide:
- what kind of bank it wants to be;
- what strategies are necessary to attain these goals;
- what effect the cost of funds will have on operating expenses;
- what uses of funds are most profitable.

In specific areas, the bank management team must decide how to structure its investment portfolio, by buying and selling securities, and deciding whether or not to purchase an interest rate SWAP to manage its interest rate risk. In the loan area, the team must decide how to price a variety of commercial and consumer loan categories, what levels to set for credit quality, and how to manage the business development and lending limits of the bank. In the deposits area, the team again must price a variety of demand and savings instruments and determine how the pricing and marketing of these instruments affects its ability to attract funds. In the overall management of the bank, each bank has additional funding sources with repurchase agreements, certificates of deposits, and additional sources of capital in the form of stock issue or long term debt. The bank management team determines its dividend level and declares an earnings forecast.

Communications

In reality, managers in one area of a bank are often unaware of the decisions made in other areas of the bank. At the Summer School, participants from one country are often unaware of the banking environment and banking policies of another country. With rapid change in economic structures and environment, participants often find themselves facing the same rapid changes in their BankExec banks as those discussed by the speakers in their papers and presentations.

Because of the volume of information provided to each bank team, and the limited amount of decision-making time available during the simulation, teams often divide responsibilities among themselves, with sub-groups making decisions individually in the investment, funding, and credit areas. Each participant has to work hard to maintain a constant awareness of the bank's goals, and what he/she must do to ensure that his/her area is co-ordinated with these goals and the other decisions made by the team.

During the Simulation

During the six quarters of the simulation, the teams are forced to deal with dramatic competitive moves, the changing economy, and the financial difficulties of the marketplace. Price wars are not uncommon as banks move quickly to capture deposits or loans. In the investment areas, traders show their colours early with speculative buying of securities, creative funding, and decisions involving SWAP transactions. Participants debate with each other, debate with other bank management teams, debate with their group leaders, and debate with the BankExec administrative team. While there are a number of challenging questions, and even a few heated exchanges, everyone moves toward improving the bank's performance and learning some interesting things about banks and their ever-changing environment.

At the End of the Simulation

When the six quarters end and the final results are distributed and posted, the participants gather to participate in a closing session. The session focuses on brief overviews of the teams' performance and on the broader issues of discovery and learning that have been achieved from the simulation. The competitive spirit is not diminished by the end of the simulation. Sparked by the IBSS athletic competitions, bank management teams have been known to try to negotiate mergers, acquisitions and hostile takeovers. The BankExec administrative team bring the simulation program to a close, with some special awards recognizing outstanding performance in a number of different areas.

Strategic Implications for Manpower Training and Productivity

Professor Amin Rajan

Director
Centre for Research in Employment
and Technology in Europe

Amin Rajan

Amin Rajan is the director of the Centre for Research in Employment and Technology in Europe (CREATE) — a pan-European network of researchers undertaking special research and consultancy assignments for the EEC and various multinational companies. He is also a visiting professor at the City University Business School and a member of the London Human Resource Group.

Before joining CREATE, he worked as an economic adviser at the National Economic Development Office, Cabinet Office and HM Treasury. From there he moved to the Institute of Manpower Studies where he was a senior research fellow.

He has carried out studies for the UK Government, as well as for international bodies such as the EEC, OECD and ILO He has also acted as a consultant to companies and published numerous books and articles on socio-economic forecasting, global developments, employment trends, new technologies, training and Europe.

Contents

1. Introduction

All the papers in this volume have the same theme but a different focus, and the thread running through them is strong but by no means obvious. How, for example, do the macro-economic developments highlighted by the Rt Hon Robin Leigh-Pemberton, Governor of the Bank of England, relate to the Midland Bank's approach to technology, outlined by Ronald Price; or to Deutsche Bank's organizational changes described by Hilmar Kopper? And is there a link between the changing nature of competition analysed by Professor Ian Morison on the one hand and the requirements of decentralised decision-making, as suggested by Lord Alexander on the other?

But an over-arching theme does emerge from all the papers. It is simply that banks face yet new challenges in the 1990s; in order to meet them successfully, banks need to make effective use of all their financial, technological and branch resources. In practical terms, it means achieving an optimal deployment of what Mr Kopper regards as a bank's "most important input asset", namely its staff.

The recent and future structural changes in the banking industry, as identified in all the papers, have strong historical parallels in the world-wide manufacturing industry in the aftermath of the 1973-74 and 1979-80 recessions. They have taught us one abiding lesson above all else: in a dynamic trading environment, the key to success is having an adaptable workforce, capable of acting as a shock absorber that at once provides a flexible response and a competitive edge. After all, financial, technological and infrastructure resources do not have an operating mechanism of their own: they are only as good as the staff who manage them.

This paper reflects on all the other papers in this volume with two objectives in mind:

■ to draw out the key human resource implications of their arguments;

■ to identify the specific actions that need to be taken, if banks are to achieve the maximum possible productivity from their staff.

That said, it is as well to emphasise at the outset that in a short paper like this one, it is impossible to do full justice to all the human resource issues touched by other papers. For the sake of brevity, I shall focus on two issues: training and productivity. Not only are they vital but they are also all-embracing, from the point of view of individual banks in the turbulent 1990s.

In order to establish the necessary linkages with the other papers, I have developed my arguments under three generic areas which have been singled out by the previous contributors as important: customisation of products, application of new technology and re-organization of corporate structures. This paper discusses them individually before drawing out the salient messages and appropriate actions in the related areas of manpower training and productivity.

2. Customisation and Rise of Knowledge Workers

The Governor puts it succinctly ". . . one lesson of the 1980s is that new products need to be tailored to identified customer needs if they are to make a durable impression". Customisation of banking products is one of the important outcomes of the so-called financial services revolution of the last decade, underpinned as it has been by deregulation, the use of revolutionary information technology and the emergence of sophisticated diverse customer groups.

The City of London, for example, best exemplifies the headlong drive towards customisation. In the early 1970s, the City's product portfolio comprised some 10 clearly identifiable services. Now, that figure stands at around 800[1]. Some, like swaps and options are genuinely new products, born out of the securitisation process associated with the new techniques of financial engineering. Others, like debt restructuring, mergers and acquisition, are old products that have been substantially repackaged to meet the specific circumstances of the client. Either way, product innovation has contributed notably to the fee and non-fee incomes of banks in all the OECD countries[2]. It looks as if customisation will remain the name of the game in the 1990s as well, in the light of three prospective developments: the creation of the single market in financial services in the European Community after 1992, further deregulation in Japan and the USA, and the Uruguay Round of GATT.

Experience from the previous wave of customisation identifies four critical success factors that have transformed mature standardised products into an array of customised ones[1]. Shown in Figure 1, they are:

- ◼ *Technology*, providing new services (eg credit cards, cash management) and new distribution channels (eg ATMs).
- ◼ *Marketing*, creating an overall environment in which customers and staff want to be actively associated with a bank, its image and its products.

Role of Know-how in Product Innovation

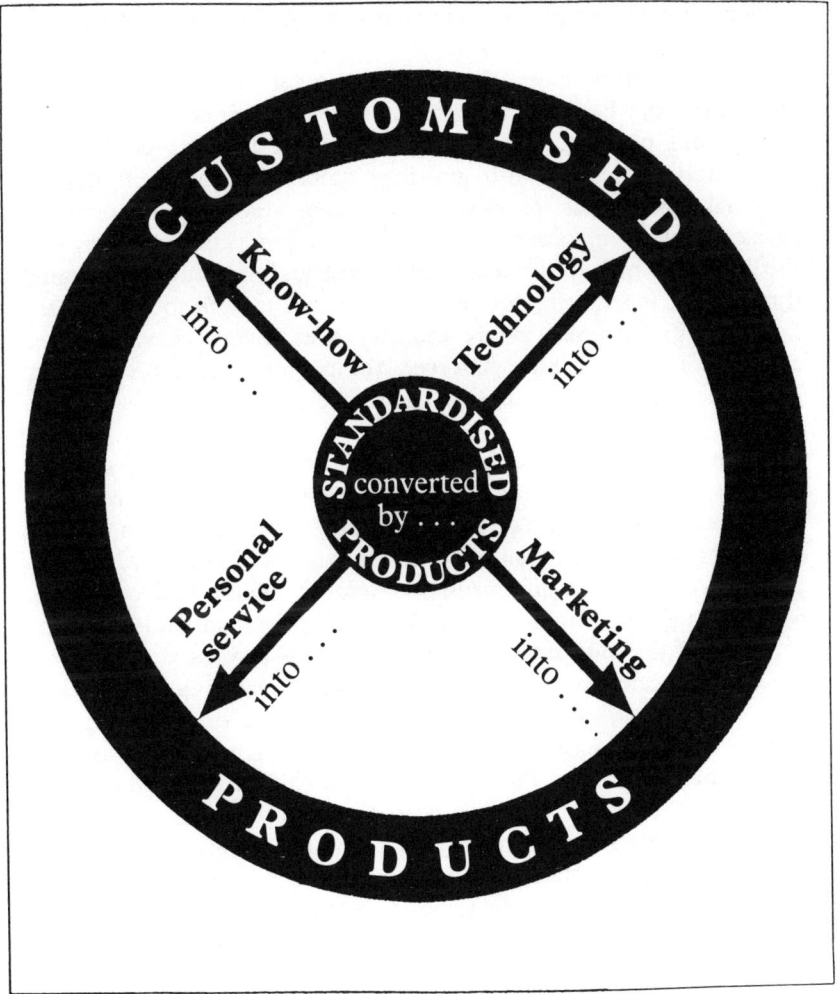

Figure 1

■ *Personal service,* aiming to improve customers' perceptions of a bank's products through friendly inter-personal encounter and informed product counselling.

■ *Know-how,* aiming to incorporate the specific characteristics of customers in diverse economic and social settings into the three conventional phases of a product cycle: design, creation and delivery.

These factors have played a prominent role in the product innovation that has occurred alongside the shift from relationship to transactions banking, taking place in the last decade. As Professor Morison has stressed, with growing competition this shift has led financial institutions to devote increasing resources to research, development, promotion and delivery of new products. He clearly sees the limits to which this process can be pushed. For example, he argues that ". . . it is tempting for established banks to seek to emulate the fast-moving consumer goods industry and invest heavily in the creation of brand values; however, the commodity nature of most banking products is bound to limit the effectiveness of such a strategy."

Not withstanding this limitation, evidence shows that banks are striving to achieve a significant measure of branding in product areas where personal service and know-how play a pivotal role in shaping consumer perceptions: areas such as, for example, contractual savings, pensions, home loans, life insurance, venture capital, project finance, asset management, multi-currency loans and private placement issues.

One of the outward manifestations of this process is the notable growth in recent and prospective demand for a new group of staff, aptly called *knowledge workers.* Aptly, because they are the new prima donnas of the finance sector as it has increasingly come to rely on three vital attributes that they possess: higher-level educational qualifications; intellectual skills geared towards problem-solving and decision-making in a fast moving market; and the ability to exercise greater discretion within decentralised structures that Lord Alexander sees as inevitable. Available forecasts of the demand for knowledge workers amply corroborate Lord Alexander's point that banks will need competent, well-trained and flexible management[1].

That begs an important question, though: why should this future demand be a matter of concern? There are two reasons. First, such demand impinges on highly scarce skills which can no longer be "vacuum cleaned" from the rest of the economy, as has been done by banks in the Anglo-Saxon and Latin countries in the last decade. Second, future knowledge workers of the type identified by Lord Alexander will have a number of important traits which the current generation of human resource managers, brought up under the classical industrial relations tradition, will find increasingly difficult to cope with. Let us pause and illustrate this by identifying one problem area: Lord Alexander argues that "Banks need a far larger number of specialists, and these are likely to have a professional loyalty as well as an employer loyalty". Yet evidence shows that such specialists have[1]:

- early work experience with large/reputable companies that makes them highly marketable;
- a high sense of self-worth, individualism, autonomy and enterprise that makes them difficult to manage;
- greater loyalty to their "craft" than to their organisations, that raises all manner of difficult issues in the area of retention and teamwork, which Mr Kopper rightly regards as essential.

Given these traits, it has proved difficult for many banks to retain, deploy and motivate their knowledge workers effectively. As a recent ILO report shows all too clearly, pay and perks in the banking industry are superior to national levels in most countries[3]. Yet problems of retention, motivation and loyalty persist. As always, there are many reasons, but the paramount one is the relative lack of clear focus in staff training. In a service environment where know-how is emerging as a prime resource, training needs to extend beyond equipping the staff with job-specific skills, as we shall see in Section 5. Before then, though, it is essential to delve into two other generic areas which have equally strong implications for training and productivity.

3. New Technology

There is little doubt that technology has transformed the banking industry in the last decade. However, as Huib Muller's paper observed "There have been enormous investments in technology, but some of this money has clearly been poorly directed." This point is borne out by widespread disenchantment with information technology[4]. No doubt sales hype on the part of the vendors unduly raised expectations on technology's promise. But there is one very good reason why the promise has yet to materialise.

The new technology opened a window of opportunity to reorganize work and organizational structures. Many banks missed the opportunity to the extent that technology merely served to perpetuate the existing arrangements. Of course, it automated many routine functions thereby reducing the cost of paper processing. But it did much less to change the social infrastructure, despite its known capability to work at a speed 200 million times faster than an average human brain.

Against the background of a headlong growth in business volume, maybe there was a less pressing need to question the validity of the existing arrangements in the first wave of technological applications. Ronald Price shows clearly that, hitherto, the central thrust of technology has been directed at automating routine processes and creating new products, both of which have helped banks to secure a cost-effective growth. He sees this process continuing into the future when banks will need ". . . to develop their own IT awareness so they can 'spot' the market niches which IT can use to exploit and also so they can play a full part in developing the products/services to fit these markets".

Although not overtly referring to organizational changes, it is clear to me that Mr Price is referring to the formulation of IT strategies within decentralised business units. As such, implicit in his analysis is the role of IT as an organizational innovation, under which there is a two-way linkage between a bank's business and organizational strategies, on the one hand, and its use of technology on the other. In this elaborate chain of causation, changes in the external environment invoke changes in organizational structures which, in turn, are facilitated by a more innovative use of technology, and this, in turn, at least partially serves to reshape the external environment. In this mutually reinforcing circle of actions and reactions, IT is viewed as supporting decentralised and flexible organizational structures with fewer hierarchies, and more rational branch networks that are directly responsive to the varying scale and nature of customer demand. Thus defined, as an organizational innovation, technology makes two demands which have to be met if the changing branch networks are to be economic:

- *New skills:* most of the banking staff need to have a set of five generic skills: procedural, technological, social, knowledge-based and entrepreneurial.
- *Hybrid skills:* specialist staff working in the IT departments need hybrid skills that specifically combine technical, business and inter-personal skills, so as to convert IT into a tool of business success,

as described by Mr Price. In banks, the hitherto ivory tower mentality of IT departments has extracted a heavy price in terms of delays, costs and rigidity of new information systems.

■ *A new value system:* all staff need to adopt work arrangements based on teamwork, trust and continuous learning as required by the circular process described earlier. In sum, this amounts to developing a new value system. The traditional value system, based on seemingly paternalistic culture, has served banks well when the market environment was stable. Now there is a need for a system that is consistent with discontinuity.

Thus, business imperatives dictate that the next generation of IT systems do not carry the same dead weight as the previous ones. As with customisation, that also means a new approach to training, which focuses on the formation of new skills as well as values.

4. Organizational Changes

The last section highlighted the role of technology in the context of organizational and environmental changes. That the market changes are remodelling corporate structures is not in doubt. As Mr Kopper has shown, even the structure of Europe's biggest universal bank was no longer sacrosanct. His case study of the Deutsche Bank is full of interesting insights about the successful management of change.

In order to provide the necessary background, however, let me digress slightly. Professor Morison sees "the deconstruction of hitherto integrated financial activities into their component parts" as an important trend of recent years. He goes on to argue that "Thus it is the cost structure, not of the business of banking as a whole, but of its myriad component parts that will increasingly determine the state of competition in the industry. This is the economics of cherry picking". He is right. Even the hitherto profitable and fast growing Japanese banks are rethinking their product and market strategies on a scale which will put extra strain on their corporate structures. This much is clear from the paper by Dr Andreas Prindl.

It is in this context that Mr Kopper's paper is especially illuminating. The logic of restructuring at the Deutsche Bank follows the circularity outlined in the last section. In that sense, the bank seems to be moving down a well-trodden path. What is notable, however, is the explicit imperative that, in the process, it ". . . had to conform to the values and the 'mission' of the Deutsche Bank" as personified by its four distinct orientations: relationship, universal, decentralisation and regional. Two options were considered: divisionalisation, creating banks within a bank; and corporate groupings, with independent profit centres sharing common services such as administration, EDP and personnel. The latter option was chosen because it conformed to the stated imperative: achieving differentiation where desirable, and integration elsewhere. He argues "After all, the aim was to shake things up whilst at the same time maintaining a measure of security and understanding. One is well aware that individuals do not do 'big things', but that teamwork still counts."

Restructuring, involving corporate groupings, has also been applied in many unpublished cases but with seemingly less success due to two reasons:

■ *Lack of clarity in corporate culture:* the burgeoning army of knowledge workers like to know what their bank's value system and mission are, partly to serve as good ground rules of behaviour, partly to provide a sense of direction and partly to act as motivators. In a service environment, these functions are vital in securing high productivity.

■ *Lack of horizontal moves:* the integration mechanism has been used to achieve economies of scale in the area of common services. That is all to the good. But it also needs to extend to horizontal movement of staff from one division to another.

Of course, the advantages of specialisation within a single area cannot be denied: indeed, in areas like mergers and acquisitions, it is a vital prerequisite for obtaining client mandate. Equally, in a fast moving environment, the disadvantage can no longer be ignored. In this context, two disadvantages are particularly noteworthy, according to a recent study[1]:

■ *Skills obsolescence:* in the event of rapid market or product change — as will be the norm in the 1990s — the acquired specialisms can be highly relevant one year and obsolete the next.

■ *Tribalism:* the existence of "banks within a bank" has promoted insularity and an "us and them" syndrome that verges on tribalism. Yes, it provides creativity and competition between individual units. All the same, it has proved dysfunctional on the whole: it has retarded teamwork and promoted the cultural diversity that run counter to the emerging need for achieving greater synergy, leverage, communication and networking between as many staff as possible.

That the scope for lateral moves does exist in many banks cannot be denied. The Japanese banks operating in London have deliberately opted for transfers of the type described in Figure 2 *(see page 186)*. In some cases, they involve dealers moving into the sales areas; in others, they involve sales specialists moving into financial engineering. The background features of staff involved in each area are shown in the larger rectangle and their skills repertoire in the smaller rectangle underneath. From that, it is clear that skills developed in one area can be used as a base on which new skills can be built.

The range of specialisms, identified by Lord Alexander and Mr Price independently, require the implementation of horizontal job moves which produce individuals with rounded experience, acquired through experiential learning and continuous training. To put their points in the new parlance of human resource management, in the 1990s banks will increasingly require two categories of staff:

- *Functional hybrids:* individuals who have acquired significant cross-fertilisation of skills through varied work experience and on-the-job training.
- *Organizational hybrids:* individuals whose varied work experience enables them to maximise overall organizational efficiency by creating greater synergy, leverage, communication and networking.

As Robin Leigh-Pemberton has argued: "Some banks will, however, inevitably and rightly continue to seek new business through product innovation, and to exploit such niches as they may thereby create for themselves." But to do so, banks will need organizational and personnel structures that are at once adaptive and productive. That means giving a high priority to the deployment of hybrid skills where it is advantageous, and specialised skills where they are relevant. Be that as it may, available forecasts show that hybrid skills will be scarce in future. Accordingly, banks themselves will need to expand their own seed-bed of such skills. That necessarily means giving a high profile to training and development — definitely on a scale that marks a notable improvement on the past performance.

5. Implications for Training and Productivity

This section draws together the salient points emerging from the analysis so far. Taking the three generic areas individually, it is clear that:

Model of Internal Transfers within a Merchant Bank

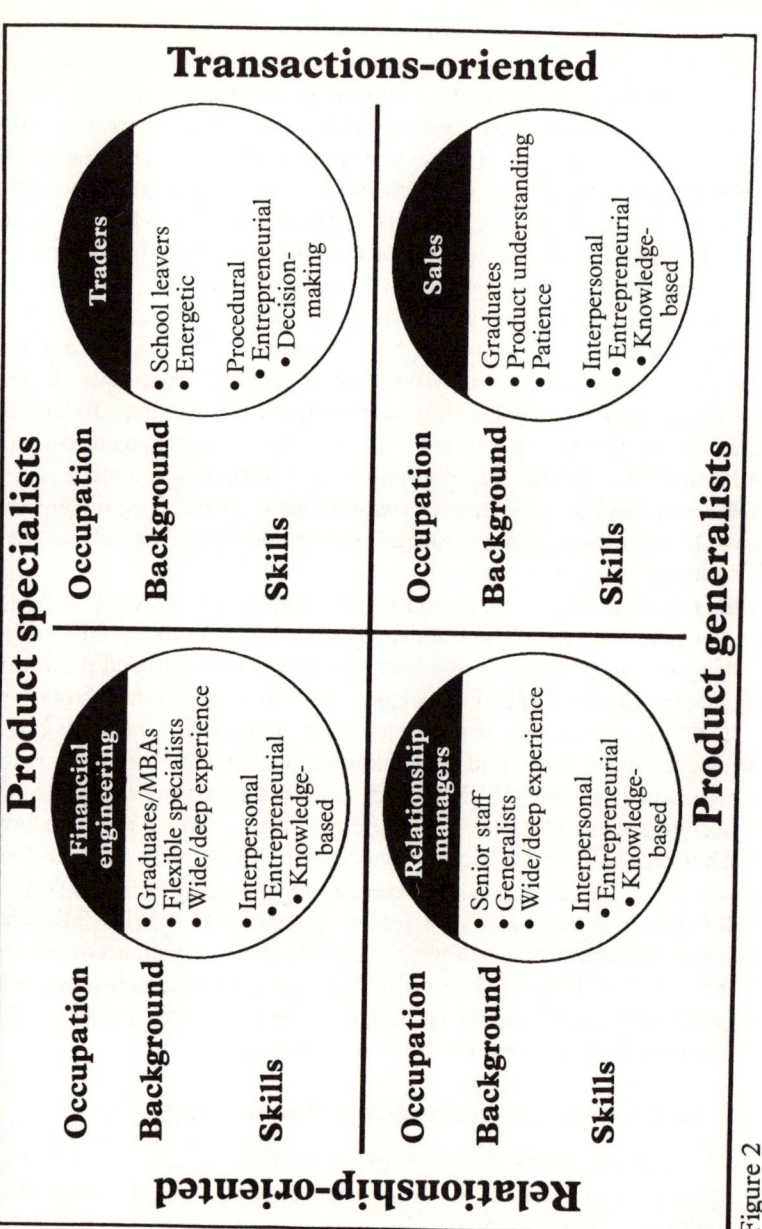

Transactions-oriented

Product specialists

Traders

Occupation

Background
- School leavers
- Energetic

- Procedural
- Entrepreneurial
- Decision-making

Skills

Sales

Occupation

Background
- Graduates
- Product understanding
- Patience

- Interpersonal
- Entrepreneurial
- Knowledge-based

Skills

Financial engineering

Occupation

Background
- Graduates/MBAs
- Flexible specialists
- Wide/deep experience

- Interpersonal
- Entrepreneurial
- Knowledge-based

Skills

Relationship managers

Occupation

Background
- Senior staff
- Generalists
- Wide/deep experience

- Interpersonal
- Entrepreneurial
- Knowledge-based

Skills

Product generalists

Relationship-oriented

Figure 2

- *Customisation* calls for a multi-strand approach to training that extends beyond equipping staff with job specific skills, whilst taking into account the special features of the knowledge workers that banks rely on and the service nature of the environment in which they operate.
- *New technology* calls for an expanded repertoire of skills and a new value system that is conducive to trust, teamwork and a learning culture.
- *Organizational changes* call for a coherent culture and experiential learning that jointly promote staff loyalty to the bank, as well as learning through varied work experience associated with lateral job moves.

These requirements have been often overlooked in the discussion on the financial services revolution. At any rate, the discussion has focused more on the *visible* features like deregulation, technology and new products; and less on *invisible* features like skills, work arrangement and culture that are the main drivers in the "engine room" of individual banks. Numerous books have appeared on the visible features, but very few on the invisible ones. The reason is quite simple: human resource management has come a long way in banking in the 1980s but it still has a long way to go, given the speed of change. Under it, two shifts are evident:

- less emphasis on growth in staff numbers and more on the quality of skills they possess;
- less emphasis on long-term career development through normal progression and more on short-term improvement in productivity.

The critical question now is quite simple: how can banks manage these shifts without jeopardising their market position? To answer the question, it is helpful to look at the past to reinforce the point made by Lord Alexander when he quotes the famous philosopher: "Those who do not learn from the past are condemned to repeat it". In order to learn from the past, it is worth dwelling on two empirical observations on banks' cost structure, as made in the previous contributions.

The first of these is made by Professor Morison when he argues that "U-shaped cost-curves may be the norm outside the United States as well as inside." On the face of it, his point runs counter to the conventional argument about economies of scale associated with size. But he does provide a convincing explanation by arguing that ". . . the business of banking is largely about the effective management of internal information flows, and the difficulty of this task increases with the size and complexity of the organization."

The second observation is provided by Mr Kopper, using findings from studies carried out by McKinsey: ". . . probably only less than a quarter of total costs can be allocated directly, 20-30 per cent being pure overhead, the remainder being unaccounted for."

To me, both the U-shaped cost curve and the unaccounted costs are symptomatic of three developments identified in other studies[1,4,6]:

- inadequate internal communication, as Professor Morison suggests;
- lack of clarity in corporate culture, such that the bank's norms and values are not obvious; and
- training being too narrow in its focus to the extent that staff are not equipped to operate at "best practice" levels of efficiency.

So, what needs to be done? Two actions recommend themselves[1].

First, banks need to ensure that their corporate culture is:

- *Motivational,* meaning that it is open, communicative and supportive to the extent that it engenders teamwork and loyalty amongst knowledge workers and others alike. In other words, a culture that overtly seeks to establish a clear mutuality of interest between the bank on the one hand and its staff on the other.
- *Integrative,* meaning that it aims to integrate as many functions within the bank as desirable so as to achieve an overall effectiveness that is greater than the sum of its parts.

Second, the banks' training effort should have triple strands. These have already been outlined in detail in another report from The Chartered Institute of Bankers[7]. Briefly, they are as follows:

- the first strand should seek to develop skills that are specific to an individual's current job;
- the second strand should seek to develop higher order thinking skills that can help to solve problems and make decisions in the current job, as well as serve as career preparation for the next one;
- the third strand should seek to develop personal attributes such as social, linguistic, teamworking and cultural skills; resulting in a better "corporate" citizen, team-player and communicator.

Evidence shows that banks all over the world are rather good on the first strand[3]. But as the financial services revolution has continued apace, issues surrounding customisation, technology and organizational structures have come to the fore; commanding due attention from senior management. Training has yet to do that on a scale that can be seen to mark visible progress. As a result, the second and third strands have yet to receive the priority that they rightly deserve. Yet, from their very nature, it is clear that they are crucial in avoiding the U-shaped cost curve as well as reducing the unaccounted costs.

6. Concluding Remarks

If banks want to improve their cost structures, training will have to become a high profile activity. After all, product, technological and organizational changes are only as good as the people who carry them out. Without the essential human ingenuity and supportive culture, these changes can never be cost-effective.

At the same time, it is essential to emphasise that the financial services revolution is radically changing the nature of work in banks. The innovative features of this revolution — like customisation and new technology — are there for all to see. What has yet to emerge on a significant scale is a training approach that not only develops the necessary skills, but also serves to achieve their optimal deployment.

The three outstanding developments in the 1990s — the single market, further deregulation in Japan and the USA and the Uruguay Round — will doubtless accelerate the revolution. For individual banks to survive and prosper in it, the seemingly benign neglect of training in the recent past has to be turned into a major concern for senior management. Otherwise, the revolution will be noted only for all the hardships that it can inflict.

Reading List

1. Amin Rajan, *Capital People,* Report from the London Human Resource Group, Industrial Society Press, London, 1990.
2. OECD, *New Financial Instruments — Disclosure and Accounting,* Paris, 1988.
3. ILO, *Multinational Banks and their Social and Labour Practices,* Geneva, 1991.
4. Amin Rajan, *Create or Abdicate: the City's Human Resource Choice for the Nineties,* Report from the London Human Resource Group, Witherby & Co Ltd, 1988.
5. Wield and Smith, "Banking on the New Technology — Choices and Constraints", *International Journal of Information Management,* Volume 7, pp 115-129.
6. Amin Rajan, *Services — The Second Industrial Revolution?,* Butterworths, 1987.
7. *Staff Development in Tomorrow's Finance Industry,* Cambridge Seminar 1989, The Chartered Institute of Bankers, 1989.

Programme

Saturday	Sunday
13 July	14 July

Saturday — 13 July

2.00-5.00pm
Arrival and Registration
(Foyer — Fisher Building)

4.00-5.30pm
Tea (Foyer)

6.30pm
Director's Reception
(Marquee — First Court)

7.30pm
Dinner (Hall)

Sunday — 14 July

8.00-9.30am
Breakfast (Buttery)

10.15am
General Briefing
(Palmerston Room)

11.00-11.15am
Coffee (Foyer)

11.15-12.30pm
Discussion Groups: Introductions
(Group rooms)

1.00pm
Lunch (Hall)

2.30-4.30pm
Tour of Colleges
(starts from main gate)

4.30-5.30pm
Tea (Foyer)

7.30pm
Dinner (Hall)

"What's Right with the World?"
After-dinner speech by
Rupert Pennant-Rae,
Editor, *The Economist*

9.30pm
National Party
Australia/New Zealand
(Marquee — First Court)

Monday

15 July

7.30-8.30am
Breakfast (Buttery)

8.45-9.45am
Paper 1: Banking in a Changing World Economy
Discussion Groups (Group rooms)

10.00-10.30am
Paper 1: Introduction by speaker,
The Rt Hon Robin Leigh-Pemberton, FCIB,
Governor of the Bank of England
(Palmerston Room)

10.30-11.00am
Coffee (Foyer)

11.00-12.30pm
Paper 1: Questions and discussion
(Palmerston Room)

1.00pm
Lunch (Hall)

2.15-3.30pm
BankExec Plenary Briefing
(Palmerston Room)

3.30-4.00pm
Tea (Foyer)

4.00-7.00pm
BankExec — Briefing and Decision 1
(Group rooms)

8.00pm
Dinner (Hall)

Tuesday

16 July

7.30-8.30am
Breakfast (Buttery)

8.45-9.45am
Paper 2: Banks and Governments: Is Supervision needed in a Deregulated Economy? by Huib Muller
Discussion Groups (Group rooms)

10.00-10.30am
Paper 2: Introduction by
Peter Hayward, Secretary, Basle Committee on Banking Supervision
(Palmerston Room)

10.30-11.00am
Coffee (Foyer)

11.00-12.30pm
Paper 2: Questions and discussion
(Palmerston Room)

1.00pm
Lunch (Hall)

"Stress" — After-lunch speech by
Dr Tom Stuttaford,
Medical Correspondent, *The Times*

3.30-4.00pm
Tea (Foyer)

4.00-6.45pm
BankExec — Decision 2 (Group rooms)

7.30pm
Dinner (Hall)

9.00pm
Presentation on Docklands by **David Hardy,** Chairman, London Docklands Development Corporation
(Palmerston Room)

9.30pm
National Party Benelux
(Marquee — First Court)

194

Wednesday	Thursday
17 July	18 July

Wednesday — 17 July

7.30-8.30am
Breakfast (Buttery)

10.00am
Coaches depart for London
(from Northampton Street)

12.30pm
Reception and lunch at Guildhall
Principal guest: **The Rt Hon
Edward Heath, MBE, MP**

Optional sightseeing in the City
of London

4.45-6.00pm
Reception at Bank of England

6.30pm
Cruise on River Thames

8.00pm
Buffet supper, Terrace Restaurant,
London Docklands Development
Corporation, Thames Quay Offices

10.30pm
Coaches depart for Cambridge

Thursday — 18 July

7.30-8.30am
Breakfast (Buttery)

8.45-9.45am
**Paper 3: Dynamics of
Competition in Banking**
Discussion Groups (Group rooms)

10.00-10.30am
Paper 3: Introduction by speaker,
Professor Ian Morison, FCIB,
Midland Group Professor of Banking
and Finance, Loughborough
University (Palmerston Room)

10.30-11.00am
Coffee (Foyer)

11.00-12.30pm
Paper 3: Questions and discussion
(Palmerston Room)

1.00pm
Lunch (Hall)

4.00-4.30pm
Tea (Foyer)

4.30-6.45pm
BankExec — Decision 3
(Group rooms)

7.30pm
Dinner (Hall)

"Business Ethics" — After-dinner
speech by **John Drummond,**
Managing Director,
Communication Works

9.00pm
National Party
Japan
(Marquee — First Court)

Friday

19 July

7.30-8.30am
Breakfast (Buttery)

8.45-9.45am
Paper 4: Organizational Changes in Banking — A Case Study
Discussion Groups (Group rooms)

10.00-10.30am
Paper 4: Introduction by speaker,
Hilmar Kopper, Spokesman of the Board of Managing Directors, Deutsche Bank
(Palmerston Room)

10.30-11.00am
Coffee (Foyer)

11.00-12.30pm
Paper 4: Questions and discussion
(Palmerston Room)

1.00pm
Lunch (Hall)

Afternoon
Sports competitions

5.00pm
Coaches depart for Newmarket Racecourse for an evening at the races — supper included
(from Northampton Street)

Saturday

20 July

7.30-8.30am
Breakfast (Buttery)

8.45-10.45am
BankExec — Decision 4
(Group rooms)

11.00am-1.00pm
Debate: **The Environment is more important than Profit**
Proposed by **Professor Ron Johnston,** Pro-Vice Chancellor for Academic Affairs and Professor of Geography, University of Sheffield
Opposed by (to be advised)
Summing-up by **Eric Glover,** Director, 44th IBSS
(Palmerston Room)

1.30pm
Lunch (Hall)

3.30-5.30pm
Garden Party
(St. John's College Backs)

7.00pm
Concert by The City Waites — an informal evening covering 400 years of music and song
(Marquee — First Court)

9.00pm
Supper
(sponsored as a National Party by the Nordic Countries — Hall/Marquee)

Sunday
21 July

8.00-9.30am
Breakfast (Buttery)

Morning Free

1.00pm
Lunch (Hall)

Afternoon
Excursions (optional) to Burleigh
House, Sandringham Estate and
Duxford Imperial War Museum
(Depart from Northampton Street)

4.30-5.00pm
Tea (Foyer)

8.30pm
Supper
(sponsored as a National Party by
USA/Canada — Hall/Marquee)

Monday
22 July

7.30-8.30am
Breakfast (Buttery)

8.45-9.45am
Paper 5: The Technology Response
Discussion Groups (Group rooms)

10.00-10.30am
Paper 5: Introduction by speaker,
Ronald Price, Managing Director,
Group Operations, Midland Bank
(Palmerston Room)

10.30-11.00am
Coffee (Foyer)

11.00-12.30pm
Paper 5: Questions and discussion
(Palmerston Room)

1.00pm
Lunch (Hall)

4.00-4.30pm
Tea (Foyer)

4.30-6.45pm
BankExec — Decision 5
(Group rooms)

7.30pm
Dinner (Hall)

9.00pm
National Party
Austria/Germany/Switzerland
(Marquee — First Court)

23 July

7.30-8.30am
Breakfast (Buttery)

8.45-9.45am
Paper 6: The Ebb and Flow of Japanese International Banking
Discussion Groups (Group rooms)

10.00-10.30am
Paper 6: Introduction by speaker,
Dr Andreas R. Prindl, FCIB, FCT, Chairman, Nomura Bank International (Palmerston Room)

10.30-11.00am
Coffee (Foyer)

11.00-12.30pm
Paper 6: Questions and discussion (Palmerston Room)

1.00pm
Lunch (Hall)

Afternoon
Industrial visits
(Depart from Northampton Street)

7.30pm
Dinner (Hall)

10.00pm
National Party
France/Italy/Portugal/Spain
(Marquee — First Court)

24 July

7.30-8.30am
Breakfast (Buttery)

8.45-10.30am
BankExec — Decision 6
(Group rooms)

10.30-11.00am
Coffee (Foyer)

11.00-12.15pm
Strategic Implications for Manpower Training and Productivity Presentation by **Amin Rajan,** Director, CREATE, **Sidney Smith,** Area Personnel Manager, First National Bank of Chicago and **Rene Eksl,** Groupe d'Etudes Sociales Techniques et Economiques (Palmerston Room) followed by group discussions (Group rooms)

12.45pm
Lunch (Hall)

2.00-3.15pm
Panel discussions led by **Amin Rajan** (Palmerston Room)

3.15-3.45pm
Tea (Foyer)

3.45-5.00pm
BankExec — concluding Plenary Session (Palmerston Room)

7.30pm
Supper (sponsored as a National Party by England, Ireland and Scotland — Marquee — First Court)

Thursday

25 July

7.30-8.30am
Breakfast (Buttery)

8.45-9.45am
Paper 7:
Developing Strategy to 2000
Discussion Groups (Group rooms)

10.00-10.30am
Paper 7: Introduction by speaker,
Lord Alexander of Weedon, QC,
FCIB, Chairman, National
Westminster Bank
(Palmerston Room)

10.30-11.00am
Coffee (Foyer)

11.00-12.30pm
Paper 7: Questions and discussion
(Palmerston Room)

1.00pm
Lunch (Hall)

Afternoon
Sports finals
(see sports booklet)

7.30pm
Farewell Dinner (Hall)

Friday

26 July

7.45-8.45am
Breakfast (Buttery)

Departure
(Coaches to Cambridge Station,
Central London and London
Heathrow Airport — details from
School Office)

198A

THE INTERNATIONAL BANKING SUMMER SCHOOL

Year	Place	Theme
1948	England	Current financial problems and the City of London
1949	England	The pattern and finance of foreign trade
1950	Sweden	Economic conditions and banking problems
1951	France	The financing of investments
1952	England	Banking and foreign trade
1953	Belgium	The recent evolution of the role of the banks in the economy
1954	Spain	The postwar functioning of banking: return to normal
1955	England	International banking and foreign trade
1956	U.S.A.	International banking and foreign trade
1957	Germany	Relations between the central banks and commercial banks
1958	Scotland	The future organisation of banking
1959	Switzerland	Financing of technical progress
1960	Netherlands	Trends in bank credit and finance
1961	England	The City of London as a centre of international trade and finance
1962	U.S.S.R.	Banking in the U.S.S.R.
1963	Austria	Commercial banks in relation to medium- and long-term credits
1964	England	Banking trends in Europe today
1965	Australia	The role of the banks in a rapidly developing economy
1966	Norway	Monetary and credit policy and the banking community
1967	Canada	Challenges and trends in modern banking
1968	Ireland	Economic planning and the banking system
1969	Denmark	Banking and the problems of economic expansion
1970	England	Banking in the 1970s
1971	Italy	Banking in a changing world
1972	U.S.A.	The world banking challenge
1973	England	The business of banking
1974	Finland	Banking in an integrating world
1975	France	New challenges for banks in today's world
1976	Australia	Banking in a changing environment
1977	Sweden	Effective use of global capital resources
1978	Belgium	Banking in the new society
1979	England	Financing of long-term development
1980	Canada	A new decade in banking
1981	West Germany	International banking: the new dimensions
1982	Scotland	The diversification of banking
1983	U.S.A.	Strategic issues for an interdependent world
1984	Netherlands	The role of the banks in international finance
1985	England	Competition and co-operation in world banking
1986	Australia	Banking in a deregulated environment
1987	Switzerland	International financial centres: structure, achievements and prospects
1988	India	Banking and economic development
1989	Ireland	Global financial services and their role in banking in the 1990s
1990	U.S.A.	The banking tightrope: prospering in an age of uncertainty